Baptistway Adult Bible Study Guide®
LARGE PRINT EDITION

Living Generously for Jesus' Sake

RONNIE AND RENATE HOOD
GARY LONG
LEIGH ANN POWERS
JEFF RAINES

BAPTISTWAYPRESS®
Dallas, Texas

Living Generously for Jesus' Sake—
BaptistWay Adult Bible Study Guide®—Large Print Edition

BAPTISTWAY PRESS® Leadership Team
Executive Director, Baptist General Convention of Texas: David Hardage
Director, Education/Discipleship Center: Chris Liebrum
Director, Bible Study/Discipleship Team: Phil Miller
Publisher, BAPTISTWAY PRESS®: Ross West

Cover and Interior Design and Production: Desktop Miracles, Inc.
Printing: Data Reproductions Corporation

First edition: June 2012

ISBN–13: 978–1–934731–90-1

How to Make the Best Use of This Issue

Whether you're the teacher or a student—

1. Start early in the week before your class meets.

2. Overview the study. Review the table of contents and read the study introduction. Try to see how each lesson relates to the overall study.

3. Use your Bible to read and consider prayerfully the Scripture passages for the lesson. (You'll see that each writer has chosen a favorite translation for the lessons in this issue. You're free to use the Bible translation you prefer and compare it with the translation chosen for that unit, of course.)

4. After reading all the Scripture passages in your Bible, then read the writer's comments. The comments are intended to be an aid to your study of the Bible.

5. Read the small articles—"sidebars"—in each lesson. They are intended to provide additional, enrichment information and inspiration and to encourage thought and application.

6. Try to answer for yourself the questions included in each lesson. They're intended to encourage further

thought and application, and they can also be used in the class session itself.

If you're the teacher—

A. Do all of the things just mentioned, of course. As you begin the study with your class, be sure to find a way to help your class know the date on which each lesson will be studied. You might do this in one or more of the following ways:

- In the first session of the study, briefly overview the study by identifying with your class the date on which each lesson will be studied. Lead your class to write the date in the table of contents on page 11 and on the first page of each lesson.

- Make and post a chart that indicates the date on which each lesson will be studied.

- If all of your class has e-mail, send them an e-mail with the dates the lessons will be studied.

- Provide a bookmark with the lesson dates. You may want to include information about your church and then use the bookmark as an outreach tool, too. A model for a bookmark can be downloaded from www.baptistwaypress.org on the Resources for Adults page.

- Develop a sticker with the lesson dates, and place it on the table of contents or on the back cover.

B. Get a copy of the *Teaching Guide*, a companion piece to this *Study Guide*. The *Teaching Guide* contains additional Bible comments plus two teaching plans. The teaching plans in the *Teaching Guide* are intended to provide practical, easy-to-use teaching suggestions that will work in your class.

C. After you've studied the Bible passage, the lesson comments, and other material, use the teaching suggestions in the *Teaching Guide* to help you develop your plan for leading your class in studying each lesson.

D. Teaching resource items for use as handouts are available free at www.baptistwaypress.org.

E. You may want to get the additional adult Bible study comments—*Adult Online Bible Commentary*—by Dr. Jim Denison (president, Denison Forum on Truth and Culture, and theologian-in-residence, Baptist General Convention of Texas). Call 1–866–249–1799 or e-mail baptistway@texasbaptists.org to order *Adult Online Bible Commentary*. It is available only in electronic format (PDF) from our website, www.baptistwaypress.org. The price of these comments is $6 for individuals and $25 for a group of five. A church or class that participates in our advance order program for free shipping can receive *Adult Online Bible Commentary* free. Call 1–866–249–1799 or see www.baptistwaypress.org to purchase or for information on participating in our free shipping program for the next study.

F. Additional teaching plans are also available in electronic format (PDF) by calling 1–866–249–1799. The price of these additional teaching plans is $5 for an individual and $20 for a group of five. A church or class that participates in our advance order program for free shipping can receive *Adult Online Teaching Plans* free. Call 1–866–249–1799 or see www.baptistwaypress.org for information on participating in our free shipping program for the next study.

G. You also may want to get the enrichment teaching help that is provided on the internet by the *Baptist Standard* at www.baptiststandard.com. (Other class participants may find this information helpful, too.) Call 214–630–4571 to begin your subscription to the printed or electronic edition of the *Baptist Standard*.

H. Enjoy leading your class in discovering the meaning of the Scripture passages and in applying these passages to their lives.

DO YOU USE A KINDLE?

This BaptistWay *Adult Bible Study Guide* plus *Profiles in Character; Amos, Hosea, Isaiah, Micah; The Gospel of Matthew; The Gospel of John: Part One; The Gospel of John: Part Two;* and *The Corinthian Letters: Imperatives for an Imperfect Church* are now available in a Kindle edition. The easiest way to find these materials is to search for "BaptistWay" on your Kindle or go to www.amazon.com/kindle and do a search for "BaptistWay." The Kindle edition can be studied not only on a Kindle but also on a PC, Mac, iPhone, iPad, Blackberry, or Android phone using the Kindle app available free from amazon.com/kindle.

AUDIO BIBLE STUDY LESSONS

Do you want to use your walk/run/ride, etc. time to study the Bible? Or maybe you're a college student who wants to listen to the lesson on your iPod®? Or maybe you're looking for a way to study the Bible when you just can't find time to read? Or maybe you know someone who has difficulty seeing to read even our *Large Print Study Guide*?

Then try our audio Bible study lessons, available on this study plus *Profiles in Character; Amos, Hosea, Isaiah, Micah; The Gospel of Matthew; The Gospel of John: Part One; The Gospel of John: Part Two;* and *The Corinthian Letters: Imperatives for an Imperfect Church*. For more information or to order, call 1–866–249–1799 or e-mail baptistway@texasbaptists.org. The files are downloaded from our website. You'll need an audio player that plays MP3 files (like an iPod®, but many MP3 players are available), or you can listen on a computer.

Writers of This Study Guide

Jeff Raines, writer of lessons one through three, is pastor, First Baptist Church, Shreveport, Louisiana. He formerly served as associate pastor, First Baptist Church, Amarillo, Texas. Dr. Raines is a graduate of Baylor University, Truett Seminary, and Princeton Seminary (D. Min.). He has served as the second vice president of the Baptist General Convention of Texas. He is a frequent writer of Bible study lessons for BaptistWay.

Leigh Ann Powers wrote lessons four through seven. This is her fourth writing assignment for BaptistWay. A mother of three, she is a graduate of Baylor University (B.S. Ed., 1998) and Southwestern Baptist Theological Seminary (M.Div., 2004). She attends First Baptist Church, Winters, Texas, where her husband, Heath, serves as pastor.

Gary Long wrote lessons eight through ten in the *Adult Bible Study Guide* and and also "Teaching Plans" for lessons eight through ten in the *Adult Bible Teaching Guide*. Gary serves First Baptist Church, Gaithersburg, Maryland, as pastor, and formerly served Willow Meadows Baptist Church, Houston, Texas. He has also served churches in North Carolina and Virginia. This is his fourth set of Bible study curriculum materials for BaptistWay.

Ronnie and Renate Hood wrote lessons eleven through thirteen in the *Adult Bible Study Guide* and also "Teaching Plans" for lessons eleven through thirteen in the *Adult Bible Teaching Guide.* Dr. Ronnie W. Hood II is pastor of Canyon Creek Baptist Church, Temple, Texas. He is a graduate of Samford University, Birmingham, Alabama. Dr. Renate Viveen Hood is associate professor of Christian Studies (New Testament and Greek) at the University of Mary Hardin-Baylor, Belton, Texas. She earned medical science degrees in the Netherlands. The Hoods studied at New Orleans Baptist Theological Seminary, where Ronnie earned M.Div., Th.M., and Ph.D. (Church History) degrees, and Renate earned M.Div. and Ph.D. (Biblical Studies and Greek) degrees.

Living Generously for Jesus' Sake

UNIT TWO

Examples That Encourage

UNIT THREE

Examples That Warn

UNIT FOUR

You Can Live Generously

Introducing

Living Generously for Jesus' Sake

The world can be divided into two kinds of people—how often we have heard that, with application to various measures for dividing people into two categories. To challenge the misuse of this statement, someone has even suggested, *The world can be divided into two kinds of people—people who divide the world into two kinds of people and people who don't.* Perhaps it is true to a degree, though, that *the world can indeed be divided into two kinds of people— givers and takers.*

The *givers* are those who tend to give generously, freely, of themselves and their possessions, and the *takers* are those who tend to guard who they are and what they have for fear they will lose either or both. *Givers* seem to approach the world from the perspective that since God can be trusted to provide generously all that is needed, they can generously share who they are and what they have with little concern about whether they themselves will run out of whatever it is they are sharing.[1] *Takers* seem to approach the world from the perspective that their resources are limited and scarce and so they must grasp them securely. When confronted with need and opportunity, *givers* spend little time calculating; rather, they just give (for examples, see Mark 14:3–9; Luke 21:1–4). *Takers*, in contrast, calculate to the penny of money and the nano-second of time. For the *giver*, the image that comes to mind is an open hand. After all, there's plenty. *Takers* can be portrayed by a clenched fist. After all, there may not be enough.

In reality, of course, dividing the world into two kinds of people is never that easy, even if doing so simplifies matters. All of us tend to be both givers and takers. We are more prone to be givers or takers in certain situations and at certain times, and less so in others. Plus, there probably are times for giving and times for not giving. We are expected to live wisely, including in our giving. There is something to be said for putting on one's own oxygen mask first, as the airline safety instructions state, so one can then be able to help others. A purpose of this Bible study is to help us to see that to be generous givers—of all of life—is the Christian way and to provide biblical guidance for learning to do that.

Generous Living

Generosity is a word that has come more and more into play in recent years to describe Christian giving—but more, Christian living. Go to a dictionary and seek definitions for "generous" or "generosity," and you'll likely find words like "openhanded," "magnanimous," "noble," "kindly," "giving freely," and even "liberal" (in a non-political sense).

How well do the definitions for "generous" or "generosity" fit God's purpose for God's people? Consider this description of the difference following Jesus made in the lives of the early Christians. It's from Justin Martyr, a second-century Christian leader and thinker. He pictured the change Jesus made like this:

> . . . We who formerly delighted in fornication, but now embrace chastity alone; we who formerly used magical arts, dedicate ourselves to the good and unbegotten God; we who valued above all things the acquisition of wealth and possessions, now bring what we have into a common stock, and communicate to every one in need; we who hated and destroyed one another, and on account of their different manners would not live with men of a different tribe, now, since the coming of Christ, live familiarly with them, and pray for our enemies, and endeavour to persuade those who hate us unjustly to live comfortably to the good precepts of Christ, to the end that they may become par-takers with us of the same joyful hope of a reward from God the ruler of all.[2]

Much about that statement shows generosity of life in action. Because of Jesus and for Jesus' sake, Christians can live generously in every area of their lives, more as givers than as takers, with the knowledge that they do not need to live in a guarded manner but in a free and open manner. Why? God himself will guard them. As the psalmist said, "The LORD is my light and my salvation, whom shall I fear? The LORD is the stronghold of my life; of whom shall I be afraid?" (Psalm 27:1).[3] As Jesus himself said of his followers, "No one will snatch them out of my hand" (John 10:28).

The God We Worship

Remember, the God we worship is a God of gracious care, whose nature is to give generously. The generous nature of our God can be seen in creation. As one commentator said so eloquently,

> . . . If you go back to Genesis, it is clear that in that beginning-less beginning, back before there was anything except God, this Mystery who is life and has life, that One must have said within himself, "This wonder of aliveness that I am, it is simply too good to keep to myself. I want others to know the ecstasy of being and of having and of doing."

... In other words, bottomless generosity is the source out of which all creation comes, and because of generosity, the truth is none of us, if we look deeply into our lives, can claim that we have earned this existence of ours by our own efforts. Each one of us [was] given life as a gift. If you look profoundly enough, birth is windfall, is coming into the possession of something that is not ours by deserving, but something that has been given to us. If we will stay in touch with that primal grace that marks the beginning of all of our lives, then the truth is we have reasons to be grateful no matter what our particular circumstances. We no longer think in terms of justice because life is not fair, because it is rooted in grace. Rather we have reason to believe that the sheer wonder of aliveness is an unending source of joy and of gratitude.[4]

We see, too, the generous nature of our God in what God has done for us in Christ. As Paul wrote, "For while we were still weak, at the right time Christ died for the ungodly. Indeed, rarely will anyone die for a righteous person—though perhaps for a good person someone might actually dare to die. But God proves his love for us in that while we still were sinners Christ died for us" (Romans 5:6–8). Or as the most well-known verse in the Bible states, "For God so loved the world that he gave his only Son, so that everyone who believes in him may not perish but may have eternal life" (John 3:16).

With such a God of generous grace caring for us and guarding us, how can we not be generous ourselves with our lives and all we have? We can live generously because of Jesus and for Jesus' sake. That is how we were meant to live. As John Claypool, the pastor and commentator just quoted about God's generous nature in creation, went on to say, "If it ever stays with us that life is gift . . . then we can begin to be generous with our lives exactly as God has been generous with God's life."[5]

Bible Studies on Living Generously

This study, *Living Generously for Jesus' Sake*, continues the annual studies of a biblical theme that BaptistWay Press® has produced for the past several years. Previous studies of biblical themes include *Growing Together in Christ, Living Faith in Daily Life, Participating in God's Mission*, and *Profiles in Character.*[6] We are grateful for the positive response to these studies even as we have continued to emphasize studies of Bible books.

Studying a biblical theme means identifying Bible passages in which that theme can be clearly seen in biblical context. This approach is considerably different from what is often called *proof-texting*, a poor approach to Bible study that can often lead one to emphasize one's own ideas rather than the scriptural message. *Proof-texting* in essence involves getting an idea and then seeking whatever scriptural justification for it can be found, generally without much attention to the context of the biblical passage. On the other hand, studying a biblical theme gives focused attention to a biblical theme as it emerges in various portions of Scripture, allowing the Scriptures to speak extensively and pointedly to this biblical theme.

The Scripture texts in this study are what one Bible scholar has called *climactic texts*—texts in which the biblical witness provides a climactic, mountain-top message on a given subject. Those are the kinds of texts on which we are focusing in this study of *Living Generously for Jesus' Sake*.

Many passages of Scripture could have been selected for the study of this biblical theme.[7] The passages selected for *Living Generously for Jesus' Sake* are to be studied in the following units and lessons.

Unit one, "Beginning with Grace," consists of three lessons that serve to remind us that God's grace is the beginning place and the sustaining strength for living generously. God's grace is seen in creation, redemption, and in daily life. We can dare to live generously because we can count on God's gracious care.

Unit two, "Examples That Encourage," contains four lessons based on life in the early church. Each lesson shows how committed believers in the early days of Christianity came to express their faith by courageously living generously and freely.

Unit three, "Examples That Warn," focuses on some of the warnings in Jesus' teachings about failing to live generously. The consequences of refusing to live generously are as tragic as the consequences of choosing to live generously are exhilarating.

Unit four, "You Can Live Generously," provides lessons on living generously in three areas of our lives. Because of our gracious, generous God, we can live generously in our relationships, with our gifts, and, yes, with our material possessions.

UNIT ONE. BEGINNING WITH GRACE

Lesson 1	Our Generous God	Genesis 1:1; Psalm 100; John 3:16; 2 Corinthians 8:8–9; Philippians 2:5–8; James 1:17–18
Lesson 2	God Cares for You	Psalms 23; 27:1–5; 116:1–9; Matthew 6:25–33
Lesson 3	Responding to Our Generous God	Psalm 116:12–19; Mark 8:34–37; 2 Timothy 1:8–12

UNIT TWO. EXAMPLES THAT ENCOURAGE

Lesson 4	God's Glad-Hearted People	Acts 2:41–47; 4:32–35
Lesson 5	Always Encouraging	Acts 4:36–37; 11:19–26; 15:36–40
Lesson 6	Giving Themselves First	1 Corinthians 16:1–4; 2 Corinthians 8:1–15; 9:6–15
Lesson 7	More Blessed to Give	Acts 20:17–35

UNIT THREE. EXAMPLES THAT WARN

Lesson 8	Greedy and Insensitive Living	Luke 12:13–21; 16:19–31; James 5:1–6
Lesson 9	Choosing Stuff over Jesus	Mark 10:17–31
Lesson 10	Failing to Be Generous	Matthew 25:31–46

UNIT FOUR. YOU CAN LIVE GENEROUSLY

Lesson 11	Be Generous in Your Relationships	Colossians 3:12–14; Hebrews 13:1–8, 14–16
Lesson 12	Be Generous with Your Gifts	1 Corinthians 12:4–31a; Ephesians 4:11–16; 1 Peter 4:10–11
Lesson 13	Be Generous with Your Money	Luke 21:1–4; 1 Timothy 6:6–10, 17–19

NOTES

1. For more on the theme of abundance and scarcity, see "The Liturgy of Abundance, the Myth of Scarcity," by Walter Brueggemann, *The Christian Century*, March 24–31, 1999. http://www.religion-online.org/showarticle.asp?title=533. Accessed 8/25/11.

2. Justin Martyr, *The First Apology of Justin*, chapter 14.http://www.earlychristianwritings.com/text/justinmartyr-firstapology.html. Accessed 9/1/11.

3. Unless otherwise indicated, all Scripture quotations in "Introducing Living Generously for Jesus' Sake," lessons 8–13, and the introductions to units 3 and 4 are taken from the New Revised Standard Version Bible.

4. John Claypool, "Life Isn't Fair, Thank God," Chicago Sunday Evening Club, January 30, 2000, program #4317. http://www.csec.org/csec/sermon/claypool_4317.htm. Accessed 8/25/11.

5. Claypool, "Life Isn't Fair, Thank God."

6. See www.baptistwaypress.org, e-mail baptistway@texasbaptists.org, or call 1–866–249–1799 for information on these studies.

7. See, for example, such Scriptures as these in addition to those identified in the lessons: 1 Chronicles 29:2–17; 2 Chronicles 31:2–12; Nehemiah 10:35–37; Psalm 49; Proverbs 11:24–25; 22:9; 28:27.

——— U N I T   O N E ———
Beginning with Grace

Unit one, "Beginning with Grace," consists of three lessons on Scriptures that serve to remind us that the beginning place and the sustaining strength for living generously is God's grace. God's grace is seen in creation, redemption, and in daily life. We can dare to live generously because we can count on God's gracious care.

UNIT ONE. BEGINNING WITH GRACE

Lesson 1	Our Generous God	Genesis 1:1; Psalm 100; John 3:16; 2 Corinthians 8:8–9; Philippians 2:5–8; James 1:17–18
Lesson 2	God Cares for You	Psalms 23; 27:1–5; 116:1–9; Matthew 6:25–33
Lesson 3	Responding to Our Generous God	Psalm 116:12–19; Mark 8:34–37; 2 Timothy 1:8–12

FOCAL TEXT

Genesis 1:1; Psalm 100;
John 3:16;
2 Corinthians 8:8–9;
Philippians 2:5–8;
James 1:17–18

BACKGROUND

Genesis 1:1; Psalm 100;
John 3:16;
2 Corinthians 8:8–9;
Philippians 2:5–8;
James 1:17–18

LESSON ONE

Our Generous God

MAIN IDEA

All the Bible reveals God's generous nature and actions in creation, redemption, and all of life.

QUESTION TO EXPLORE

Is the God you believe in uncaring, stingy, or generous?

STUDY AIM

To acknowledge God's generous nature and actions and to state what God's generosity means for my life

QUICK READ

From beginning to end, the Bible confirms that God is a giving God. We see this aspect of God most clearly through the life and sacrifice of Jesus.

As important as it is to know what we believe about God, we also need to be clear about what we *do not* believe about God. New Testament scholar N. T. Wright shared a dialogue he had with students while serving as a chaplain at Worcester College, Oxford, England. He wrote that each year he met with the new students to get to know them and welcome them.

> . . . Most were happy to meet me; but many commented, often with slight embarrassment, "You won't be seeing much of me; you see, I don't believe in god."
>
> I developed [a] stock response: "Oh, that's interesting; which god is it you don't believe in?" This used to surprise them. . . . So they would stumble out a few phrases about the god they said they did not believe in: a being who lived up in the sky, looking down disapprovingly at the world, occasionally "intervening" to do miracles. . . . Again, I had a stock response for this very common statement of "spy-in-the-sky" theology: "Well, I'm not surprised you don't believe in that god. I don't believe in that god either."[1]

Misconceptions and divine caricatures of God abound. Televangelists can leave the impression of a greedy and needy God. Others may think of God as humanity writ large, that is, petty, jealous in the worst sense, selfish, and grasping. The Bible, however, from beginning to end, paints a very different picture. At the core of God's relationship with us lies a relentless and consistent generosity.

In his imaginative work, *The Screwtape Letters*, C.S. Lewis constructed correspondence among demons about the best ways to tempt humans. He described the demonic goal as *absorption*. They take others and draw them in—absorbing them and their power to increase Satan's own. Think of the shattered, dominated life of the Gerasene man in Luke 8. His body and mind were in utter slavery to the "Legion" of demons until Jesus set him free (Luke 8:30).

Yahweh's goal is the opposite of absorbing others. God *gives* life and freedom. God desires to liberate us from those things that enslave us so that we can be the people he made us to be. "It was for freedom that Christ set us free; therefore keep standing firm and do not be subject again to a yoke of slavery" (Galatians 5:1).[2]

GENESIS 1:1

In the beginning God created the heavens and the earth.

PSALM 100

1 Shout joyfully to the Lord, all the earth.

2 Serve the Lord with gladness;
Come before Him with joyful singing.

3 Know that the LORD Himself is God;
It is He who has made us, and not we ourselves;
We are His people and the sheep of His pasture.

4 Enter His gates with thanksgiving
And His courts with praise.
Give thanks to Him, bless His name.

5 For the LORD is good;
His lovingkindness is everlasting
And His faithfulness to all generations.

JOHN 3:16

For God so loved the world, that He gave His only begotten Son, that whoever believes in Him shall not perish, but have eternal life.

2 CORINTHIANS 8:8–9

8 I am not speaking this as a command, but as proving through the earnestness of others the sincerity of your love also. 9 For you know the grace of our Lord Jesus

Christ, that though He was rich, yet for your sake He became poor, so that you through His poverty might become rich.

PHILIPPIANS 2:5–8

[5] Have this attitude in yourselves which was also in Christ Jesus, [6] who, although He existed in the form of God, did not regard equality with God a thing to be grasped, [7] but emptied Himself, taking the form of a bond-servant, [and] being made in the likeness of men. [8] Being found in appearance as a man, He humbled Himself by becoming obedient to the point of death, even death on a cross.

JAMES 1:17–18

[17] Every good thing given and every perfect gift is from above, coming down from the Father of lights, with whom there is no variation or shifting shadow. [18] In the exercise of His will He brought us forth by the word of truth, so that we would be a kind of first fruits among His creatures.

Ex Nihilo (From Nothing) (Genesis 1:1)

The first thought of the Bible in Hebrew is literally, *in beginning, God*. God's first recorded action is creation. "In the beginning God *created* the heavens and the earth" (Genesis 1:1, italics added for emphasis). One of the earliest Christian doctrines about creation is that God created *ex nihilo* (Latin for *from nothing*). God did not, like a tinkerer, order the material that was already lying around. Rather, God created out of nothing.

Only an artist can transform a blank canvas into something inspiring and captivating. Likewise, God's universe is a masterpiece of beauty, complexity, and sharing. The first verse of Scripture describes God like the source of a great river—by his very nature sharing an ever-flowing torrent of life.

Shout to the Lord (Psalm 100)

The psalms celebrate the graciousness of God's nature over and over again. Psalm 100 describes a worship scene, with the congregation outside the temple singing and shouting praise and thanksgiving to God. The reason for this jubilation is God's gracious nature. This nature should spark praise beyond the confines of Israel, since God's goodness reaches "all the earth" (Psalm 100:1). The psalmist described the expressions of God's love in God's creation of humanity, in God's shepherding care (Ps. 100:3), and in God's nature of goodness, lovingkindness, and faithfulness (100:5).

"Lovingkindness" is the Hebrew word *hesed*—one of the most common descriptions of what we find at the heart of God. It wraps together the ideas of covenant, love, faithfulness, commitment, and kindness. This psalm assures us that these things are abundant in the divine nature. We need not worry about diminishing returns or scarce resources. The supply is everlasting, and God's faithfulness will remain as long as one generation succeeds another.

A Depth of Love (John 3:16)

The New Testament bears powerful witness to God's generosity and graciousness in recording and celebrating God's fullest revelation of himself in Jesus Christ. One of Scripture's most famous verses confirms these aspects of God's nature. In the midst of his conversation with Nicodemus, a "ruler of the Jews" (John 3:1) and "teacher of Israel" (3:10), Jesus pushed the focus beyond Israel. God's love is for "the world" (3:16).

The nature of this love surpasses expectations. Most dictionaries define love with words of affection, feeling, passion, or desire. God's love, however, is defined by a boundless depth of self-sacrificial giving. God's love for

us is not confined to divine feelings but was displayed in
the great act of generosity: the giving of the "only begotten Son" (3:16).

Role Reversal (2 Corinthians 8:8–9)

In addition to seeing the Father's willingness to give the
Son for us, we find the character of generosity in Jesus
himself. In 2 Corinthians 8, Paul used Jesus' example as
he sought to inspire the Corinthians to give for the offering for the Jerusalem church. While their participation
was assumed in 1 Corinthians 16:1–4, their enthusiasm
had seemingly waned.

First, Paul appealed to the example of the churches
in Macedonia, who gave out of their own poverty
(2 Corinthians 8:1–2). Then, in verse 9 he turned to the
ultimate example of Jesus, who displayed this special
nature of God. Rather than acting to increase his own
power at the expense of others, Jesus gave profoundly and
completely for the benefit of others.

Downward Mobility (Philippians 2:5–8)

In Philippians 2, Paul captured clearly and powerfully the
attitude of giving. This language pushes beyond what we
normally understand as *generous*.

We tend to evaluate the generosity of others based on the absolute amounts given. Evidence of such evaluation is the naming of such things as buildings and libraries after wealthy donors who give tremendous amounts. Jesus evaluated gifts, however, on the amount that was left. The widow he commended in Luke 21:1–4 gave much less in absolute terms than the rich of her day, but the sacrifice of her gift caught the Savior's eye.

Perhaps Jesus saw a reflection of himself in her giving. He did not give only a little of the excess of his heavenly holdings. He did not offer a percentage of what he had to cover the sins of humanity. The language goes far beyond that. Jesus "emptied himself" (Philippians 2:7).

If someone had told us before it occurred that God would take on flesh and live among us, we would have been shocked and amazed. We probably would have imagined a figure so compelling that he would dwell in the greatest of palaces, with the kings of the entire world bringing tribute. If Jesus had come in such a way, we likely would still celebrate his humility of releasing heaven to take on flesh. Paul recounted, however, a very different model of incarnation. Jesus took the very form—the essence—of a slave. His downward mobility did not end there, for Jesus was obedient to death. His death was not just any death, but "death on a cross" (Phil. 2:8). This was the death of the despised, the condemned, and the cursed.

If our picture of God is of a demanding and grasping deity, we have missed entirely the meaning of Jesus' life.

Jesus held nothing back as he gave himself to complete and utter emptiness for you and me. He had nothing left to give. Here we find the clearest evidence for the essential nature of God's generosity.

Every Perfect Gift (James 1:17–18)

In his epistle, James beautifully highlighted the giving heart of God as he addressed one of the most fundamental life questions. Do such things as struggles, hardships, testing, and persecution come from God? James 1:13 answers the question with a definitive *no*. God does not tempt us to evil, scheming against us and delighting in our failures. The problem lies with our own evil desires, which give birth to sin and result in death (James 1:15). These wounds are self-inflicted.

James reminds us that God's nature is constant and sure as a giver of good things and "every perfect gift" (1:17). Verse 17 mentions "lights" and "shifting shadows." Some scholars see here a reference to heavenly bodies and to the belief of some that human fortunes are determined by the alignment of the planets or stars.[3] James left no room for such an appeal to fate. Our giving God is the "Father of lights," and his loving desire is for a very different progression to take place in us than the downward spiral of verse 15. Rather, God freely chose to give us life and desires that we thrive as his "first fruits" (1:18).

Conclusion

Occasionally you might hear the phrase that a company or nation or product *sucks all the oxygen out of the room.* That image captures the essence of a cut-throat, zero-sum game, in which success leaves competitors gasping on the sidelines, with only one winner.

The biblical picture of God is the complete opposite. God gives from beginning to end, wholly and completely. Scripture's final image confirms it. In the depiction of the new heaven and the new earth in Revelation 21—22, God's throne is the source of "a river of the water of life, clear as crystal" (Revelation 22:1). God is a giver for eternity.

This Lesson and Life

Philippians challenges us to a Christ-shaped life with the words, "Have this attitude in yourselves which was also in Christ Jesus" (Phil. 2:5). Instead of grasping equality with God, Jesus emptied himself.

Life presents us with abundant opportunities to choose Jesus' path over a grasping one. Very basic things reveal our hearts. Do we spend most of our time on our own pursuits, ambitions, and entertainment, or do we invest our lives in ministry to others? Do we max out every ounce of income for consumption and for our own needs and desires, or do we give generously as our giving God gives? It takes a bold, counter-cultural stand to resist our culture, which may be defined by its grasping nature. The alternative, clear in Scripture, is the example of God's love through Christ.

KENOSIS

In Philippians 2, we learn that instead of grasping equality with God, Jesus emptied himself. The Greek word for emptying, *kenosis,* has become an important term in theology for understanding the degree of God's giving nature. In many ways, creation itself was a *kenotic* act of God. In creating us and giving us freedom, God chose to limit himself. Philippians 2 describes the *kenosis* of the incarnation.

The glory of Jesus' heavenly existence lies far beyond our imaginative reach. C.S. Lewis attempted to describe the degree of *kenosis* in the incarnation in *Mere Christianity.* Lewis wrote, "The Eternal Being, who knows everything and created the whole universe, became not only a man but (before that) a baby, and before that a *foetus* inside a Woman's body. If you want to get the hang of it, think how you would like to become a slug or a crab."[4] Our God empties himself in radical *kenosis.* Do you?

MISSIONAL CHURCH

One of the important concepts about the church in recent years is the idea that a church should be *missional*. The term has come to mean different things to different people, but one important element is the idea that *sending* is at the heart of the church. Even as we seek to draw others to our churches to know the truth and hope of the gospel, how can we follow Jesus' example of giving in our sending?

QUESTIONS

1. What are some ways in which God is a giver?

2. What does it mean today that God loves this world?

3. Do you think or act as if good things in your life
   come from someone or something other than God?

4. How can you imitate our giving God?

N O T E S

1. N.T. Wright, "Jesus and the Identity of God," *Ex Auditu* (1998): 44.

2. Unless otherwise indicated, all Scripture quotations in lessons 1–7 and the introductions to units 1 and 2 are taken from the 1995 update of the New American Standard Bible®.

3. Ralph Martin, *James*, Word Biblical Commentary, vol. 48 (Waco, TX: Word Books, 1988), 42.

4. C.S. Lewis, *Mere Christianity* (New York, New York: HarperCollins Press, 2001), 179.

FOCAL TEXT

Psalms 23; 27:1–5; 116:1–9;
Matthew 6:25–33

BACKGROUND

Psalms 23; 27; 116:1–9;
Matthew 6:25–34

LESSON TWO

God Cares for You

MAIN IDEA

God's generosity is expressed in his continual, deep care for people and their needs.

QUESTION TO EXPLORE

How do you think God feels about you?

STUDY AIM

To list the ways in which these passages show God cares for people and their needs, and to state what God's care means for my life

QUICK READ

The Bible's promises are clear. Our generous God cares for you. God wants us to experience his love, compassion, provision, and freedom.

In the grand scheme of things, we are very small. Each of us is just one seven-billionth of the world's population. Our sun is just one of 400 billion stars in the Milky Way galaxy, and astronomers estimate the universe to contain 100 billion galaxies![1] The expanse of God's universe is mind-boggling, and to say that humanity's exploration has even scratched the surface would be an exaggeration. One effort, Voyager 1, was launched on September 5, 1977. It completed its primary mission, exploration around Jupiter and Saturn, in less than four years and has just kept going. By 1989, it had transmitted information about Uranus and Neptune and was hurtling out of our solar system at about 40,000 miles per hour. Before leaving, however, NASA engineers sent the command for Voyager 1 to turn and take a picture of the best-known object in the universe—the earth. Like teenagers reaching out with the camera aimed back at themselves, humanity reached out six billion kilometers and snapped a self-portrait. The resulting picture was named by Carl Sagan, "The Pale Blue Dot."[2] Our earth appears as a single pixel, caught in a ray of light from the sun.

With such a perspective, we can share the psalmist's amazement at the contrast between our place in the universe and God's care for us: "When I consider Your heavens, the work of Your fingers, The moon and the stars, which You have ordained; What is man that You take thought of him, And the son of man that You care for him?" (Psalm 8:3–4). The Bible speaks clearly about

God's concern for you. While we may each be a tiny fraction of the population of a pale blue dot, we are of concern to our Creator, whose love is still more vast than the universe he created.

PSALM 23

1 The LORD is my shepherd,
   I shall not want.
2 He makes me lie down in green pastures;
   He leads me beside quiet waters.
3 He restores my soul;
   He guides me in the paths of righteousness
   For His name's sake.
4 Even though I walk through the valley of the
   shadow of death,
   I fear no evil, for You are with me;
   Your rod and Your staff, they comfort me.
5 You prepare a table before me in the presence of
   my enemies;
   You have anointed my head with oil;
   My cup overflows.
6 Surely goodness and lovingkindness will follow me
   all the days of my life,
   And I will dwell in the house of the LORD forever.

Psalm 27:1–5

1 The Lord is my light and my salvation;
   Whom shall I fear?
   The Lord is the defense of my life;
   Whom shall I dread?
2 When evildoers came upon me to devour my flesh,
   My adversaries and my enemies, they stumbled
      and fell.
3 Though a host encamp against me,
   My heart will not fear;
   Though war arise against me,
   In spite of this I shall be confident.
4 One thing I have asked from the Lord, that I shall
      seek:
   That I may dwell in the house of the Lord all the
      days of my life,
   To behold the beauty of the Lord
   And to meditate in His temple.
5 For in the day of trouble He will conceal me in His
      tabernacle;
   In the secret place of His tent He will hide me;
   He will lift me up on a rock.

PSALM 116:1–9

¹ I love the LORD, because He hears
   My voice and my supplications.
² Because He has inclined His ear to me,
   Therefore I shall call upon Him as long as I live.
³ The cords of death encompassed me
   And the terrors of Sheol came upon me;
   I found distress and sorrow.
⁴ Then I called upon the name of the LORD:
   "O LORD, I beseech You, save my life!"
⁵ Gracious is the LORD, and righteous;
   Yes, our God is compassionate.
⁶ The LORD preserves the simple;
   I was brought low, and He saved me.
⁷ Return to your rest, O my soul,
   For the LORD has dealt bountifully with you.
⁸ For You have rescued my soul from death,
   My eyes from tears,
   My feet from stumbling.
⁹ I shall walk before the LORD
   In the land of the living.

MATTHEW 6:25–33

²⁵ "For this reason I say to you, do not be worried about your life, as to what you will eat or what you will drink; nor

for your body, as to what you will put on. Is not life more than food, and the body more than clothing?

26 "Look at the birds of the air, that they do not sow, nor reap nor gather into barns, and yet your heavenly Father feeds them. Are you not worth much more than they?

27 "And who of you by being worried can add a single hour to his life?

28 "And why are you worried about clothing? Observe how the lilies of the field grow; they do not toil nor do they spin,

29 yet I say to you that not even Solomon in all his glory clothed himself like one of these.

30 "But if God so clothes the grass of the field, which is alive today and tomorrow is thrown into the furnace, will He not much more clothe you? You of little faith!

31 "Do not worry then, saying, 'What will we eat?' or 'What will we drink?' or 'What will we wear for clothing?'

32 "For the Gentiles eagerly seek all these things; for your heavenly Father knows that you need all these things.

33 "But seek first His kingdom and His righteousness, and all these things will be added to you.

Our Loving Shepherd (Psalm 23)

One of the best-known reflections on the theme of God's care is Psalm 23. The great preacher Henry Ward Beecher (1813–1887) commented on this psalm:

David has left no sweeter Psalm than the short twenty-third. It is but a moment's opening of his soul; but, as when one, walking the winter street sees the door opened for someone to enter, and the light streams a moment forth, and the forms of children are running to greet the comer, and genial music sounds, though the door shuts and leaves the night black, yet it cannot shut back again all that the eyes, the ear, the heart, and the imagination have seen—so in this Psalm, though it is but a moment's opening of the soul, are emitted truths of peace and consolation that will never be absent from the world.[3]

These truths reveal an important aspect of God's gracious care. God wants the best for us. In fact, God wants for us what we may not recognize we need.

The image of shepherd is important in Scripture. Think of key figures of the Old Testament who worked as shepherds: Abraham, Isaac, Jacob, Moses, David. Shepherding came to be used as a term for the relationship between leaders and the people. For example, Ezekiel 34 condemns the wicked shepherds who had abused God's people. Ezekiel prophesied of the day when, "I Myself will search for my sheep and seek them out" (Ezekiel 34:11).

Drawing on this image, the psalmist started with a declaration of Lordship and its result, "The Lord is my shepherd, I shall not want" (Psalm 23:1). Our culture might write its own psalm: *I am my own shepherd, and I have wants beyond number.* What follows the psalmist's declaration is a beautiful image of *shalom*, the Hebrew word for deep and abiding peace. Sheep in ancient Israel faced dangers from theft, predators, drought, hunger, thirst, and flooded rivers. They were entirely dependent on shepherds for protection. The images of green pastures and quiet waters promise both protection and provision. God will not abandon us. God will provide.

Beyond physical needs, God speaks peace to our soul and leads us in his ways (Ps. 23:3). In life's darkest days, when hope is gone and when death itself stalks us, the God of comfort is even there (23:4). The "rod" was a weapon of protection, and the "staff" was the shepherd's tool for leading sheep. Even when enemies encircle, God is there with what is needed. Skeptics today sneer that God is a crutch and that faith limits or constricts us. On the contrary, full life comes with the proper relationship between creature and Creator. We find freedom in him from the destructive and belittling desires of our culture. We are filled to overflowing and live with the confidence that God's gracious love will be there all the way to the end (23:6).

Our Refuge (Psalm 27)

Several other psalms meditate on the theme of God's care for us. Using military imagery, the opening verses of Psalm 27 declare a profound confidence in the loving care of God. The Lord is light, salvation, and refuge. By definition, light dispels darkness. Like the "valley of the shadow" in Psalm 23, the psalmist here knows that no situation is too dark for God. The Lord as salvation points to victory. No matter the odds arrayed against us, God is able to bring about our salvation. The third reference to God describes him as refuge, stronghold, or defense. No other retreat is necessary, for God is strong enough to protect us. With such a God, the psalmist can ask with confidence, "Whom shall I dread" (27:1)? The answer is obvious: no one. This confidence comes from God's salvation in the past (27:2) and provides an unshakable foundation, no matter the odds, for whatever comes in life.

As the psalm continues in verse 4, God's generosity sparks a desire for an even deeper relationship. The psalmist wanted to behold more clearly the beauty of the Lord and to enjoy the ongoing presence of God. This presence is the source of protection, security, and hope (27:5).

Our Savior (Psalm 116:1–9)

In Psalm 116, the recital of God's care emanates from gratitude of rescue from death. Verse 3 describes the dire straits of being caught in death's trap, like prey caught by a hunter. We are not able to see the situation clearly, although verses 10–11 mention affliction and the lying of men. Many psalms of thanksgiving omit the specific situation, allowing the hymn to be used in a wider variety of contexts. What we can see clearly, however, is that when all seemed lost, the psalmist cried to God for rescue and was saved (116:4). This results in a simple and unusual declaration of love for God in verse 1. While one of the most well-known commands of Scripture is to "love the LORD your God" (Deuteronomy 6:5), the first-person statement, "I love the LORD," is rare. It appears only one other time in the psalms (Ps. 18:1), where a different verb is used.[4] The reason for this love is clear: God hears. This faith in God's attentiveness is recited over and over in 116:1, 2, and 4. We can pray with confidence because God listens to us.

God not only listens; God also acts. Verse 5 catalogues the awesome elements of God's nature that flow in blessings to us. God is gracious, righteous, and compassionate. We should not let that list fly by without considering how unusual this combination of traits appears together. Some people may be very gracious and compassionate, but they allow principles of justice and righteousness to slip. They may end up with an anything-goes attitude. On the other side are the pharisaical ones, who focus on justice or righteousness to the neglect of mercy. God, in his dealings with us, manages both and bestows both.

Verses 6–9 repeat the wonder of the psalmist at his deliverance. God's concern is not limited to important people, for he "preserves the simple" (116:6). God has transformed the psalmist's situation from one of death, tears, and stumbling to one of rest and the ability to "walk before the Lord in the land of the living" (116:9).

Our Provider (Matthew 6:25–33)

Jesus spoke about God's care for us in his broader discussion of money in the Sermon on the Mount. Verses 19–24 set up contrasting ways of life. One is a life with "mammon" as master, marked by anxiety and the accumulation on earth of things that will not last. The other recognizes God as master and focuses on "treasures in heaven" (Matthew 6:20). Like Psalm 23, where blessings flow from having the right Lord, Jesus paints the picture of God's care for those who follow him.

Jesus used mini-parables from nature with birds and flowers to call disciples to trust and faith. The birds and flowers have food and clothing, and God loves people more than birds or flowers. Therefore one should not worry about food or clothing. God will provide. Some might object that we can certainly find people without the necessities of life—believers and unbelievers alike. Does this mean God is unfaithful? It may instead mean that we are not faithful. God has graciously provided an earth with abundance to meet our needs. Those of us with much are called to be stewards and to share in God's provision.

Jesus does not want us to live anxious, needy lives that are fixated on possessions and possessed by them. He desires our freedom from worry. We can seek the main thing—God's kingdom—and live in trust and faith that he will provide what we truly need.

Implications and Actions

The passages in this lesson describe the generosity of God flowing to us in a number of ways. What does God's care and concern mean for our lives? Jesus captured the implications clearly for us in Matthew 6. "For this reason I say to you, do not be worried about your life" (Matt. 6:25). The *therefore* of God's loving care is a life of trust and faith in him. The opposite of such faith and trust is worry. Many have pointed out that worry is a form of atheism. In worrying we reveal a lack of confidence in the power and provision of our loving God. Our God cares for us and is powerful to provide all we need.

SHALOM

Our culture tends to stress choice, variety, individuality, and limitless options. From careers, to hobbies, to media, to relationships, to varieties of blue jeans we often define freedom as having no limits in the options before us.

Several of the passages in today's lesson, however, call for a narrowing of focus, vision, and purpose. In Psalm 23, the shepherd encourages us to enjoy what is truly important and beneficial. In Psalm 27, the psalmist's response to salvation is a narrowing of focus to "one thing I have asked of the Lord" (27:4). Jesus calls us to stop worrying about our life and to "seek first His kingdom and His righteousness" (Matt. 6:33). The result of living in trust and focusing on the right thing is the deep and abiding peace of God—*shalom* in Hebrew. *Shalom* extends far beyond the idea of peace as the absence of conflict. *Shalom*, rather, describes restoration, wholeness, and a sense of rightness with God.

LIFE APPLICATION

- When you feel yourself starting to worry, use that as a signal to pray. Take the matter to God.

- Make sure you remember and record God's saving acts for you. The memory of God's rescue and faithfulness can carry us through difficult times.

- Make sure your management of time, money, and other resources reflects your "seeking first" God's kingdom.

QUESTIONS

1. Do you tend to worry more about the past or the future?

2. How has God delivered you in the past?

3. Does having an abundance of wants (Ps. 23:1) tend to conflict with peace in your life?

4. Do you depend more on yourself or on God?

NOTES

1. Carl Sagan, *Pale Blue Dot: A Vision of the Human Future in Space* (New York, New York: Ballentine Books, 1994), 7, 11, 26.

2. You can see the picture online at http://visibleearth.nasa.gov/view_rec.php?id=601. Accessed 1/4/2012.

3. Henry Ward Beecher in Charles Spurgeon, *The Treasury of David, Vol.1* (Lynchburg, VA: The Old-Time Gospel Hour), 357.

4. The word "love" in Psalm 18 has roots in the ideas of mercy and compassion. "Love" in Psalm 116 bears more of the ideas of affection, family, and feelings of passion.

FOCAL TEXT

Psalm 116:12–19;
Mark 8:34–37;
2 Timothy 1:8–12

BACKGROUND

Psalm 116; Mark 8:27–37;
2 Timothy 1:1–12

LESSON THREE

Responding to Our Generous God

MAIN IDEA

God's gracious generosity calls for the generous commitment of all of life.

QUESTION TO EXPLORE

How shall we respond to God's unbelievably gracious generosity?

STUDY AIM

To describe the response God's generosity calls for and to evaluate how I have responded

QUICK READ

The Scriptures call us to respond to God's great generosity by committing our whole lives to him. As God gave all, we are to give all.

How do you react to a gift? If it has come out of the blue, we may react with surprise. Other gifts are expected—we may have chosen them ourselves—and so perhaps we respond with mock surprise. One member of our family who always had her camera out and ready when we opened Christmas gifts created some pressure when opening the gift from her. You knew that whatever registered on your face—gratitude, incomprehension, or puzzlement—would remain as a memento for all to see.

What is our response, though, to a massive gift? The long-running television show, *Extreme Makeover: Home Edition,* remodels or builds a home for someone facing special needs or circumstances. The recipient family receives a vacation, and the work is done while they are gone. The climax of the show comes with the family's return and their reaction to such an incredible gift.

The Bible gives us a record of God's great generosity. In creating, protecting, and sustaining all things, God truly is the author of life. The greatest gift of all, though, is stated so clearly in John 3:16, "For God so loved the world, that He gave His only begotten Son, that whoever believes in Him shall not perish, but have eternal life." With some gifts, a simple word of thanks will do. With others a note is required. How do we respond, however, to a generosity like God's? As God gave all, our response is to give all in return.

PSALM 116:12–19

12 What shall I render to the LORD
For all His benefits toward me?
13 I shall lift up the cup of salvation
And call upon the name of the LORD.
14 I shall pay my vows to the LORD,
Oh may it be in the presence of all His people.
15 Precious in the sight of the LORD
Is the death of His godly ones.
16 O LORD, surely I am Your servant,
I am Your servant, the son of Your handmaid,
You have loosed my bonds.
17 To You I shall offer a sacrifice of thanksgiving,
And call upon the name of the LORD.
18 I shall pay my vows to the LORD,
Oh may it be in the presence of all His people,
19 In the courts of the LORD's house,
In the midst of you, O Jerusalem.
Praise the LORD!

MARK 8:34–37

34 And He summoned the crowd with His disciples, and said to them, "If anyone wishes to come after Me, he must deny himself, and take up his cross and follow Me.

35 "For whoever wishes to save his life will lose it, but whoever loses his life for My sake and the gospel's will save it.

36 "For what does it profit a man to gain the whole world, and forfeit his soul?

37 "For what will a man give in exchange for his soul?

2 TIMOTHY 1:8–12

8 Therefore do not be ashamed of the testimony of our Lord or of me His prisoner, but join with me in suffering for the gospel according to the power of God,

9 who has saved us and called us with a holy calling, not according to our works, but according to His own purpose and grace which was granted us in Christ Jesus from all eternity,

10 but now has been revealed by the appearing of our Savior Christ Jesus, who abolished death and brought life and immortality to light through the gospel,

11 for which I was appointed a preacher and an apostle and a teacher.

12 For this reason I also suffer these things, but I am not ashamed; for I know whom I have believed and I am convinced that He is able to guard what I have entrusted to Him until that day.

Salvation Song (Psalm 116:12–19)

Lesson two explored the deliverance recorded in the first part of Psalm 116. God graciously rescued the psalmist from the brink of death. "The cords of death encompassed me and the terrors of Sheol came upon me; I found distress and sorrow" (Psalm 116:3). The Lord intervened and saved his life. The last half of the psalm then seeks to answer the question, "What shall I render to the LORD for all His benefits toward me?" (Ps. 116:12).

The first answer, "I shall lift up the cup of salvation" (116:13) refers to a worship setting. The Old Testament describes drink offerings of wine poured on the altar. For example, Jacob, in response to an appearance of God, built a stone altar and poured wine and oil on it as an offering (Genesis 35:14). Several passages in the law codes describe the practice (Exodus 29:38–41; Leviticus 23:13; and Numbers 15:5). A surprising aspect of the Hebrew text—not captured in our English translations—is that salvation is plural, *salvations* (Ps. 116:13). The worship of the psalmist, in offering this sacrifice, expressed thanksgiving for all of God's saving acts—past, present, and future. His sacrifice and proclamation in worship celebrated the graciousness woven deeply into the nature of God. This response of worship recurs in verses 17–19 with the language of a thanksgiving sacrifice and paying vows. The psalmist would stand in the temple and testify before all people that God saves and is worthy of worship, thanksgiving, and praise.

The other answer to the question of verse 12 lies in a three-fold commitment of Lordship in verse 16. How often, in times of trouble and distress, do we bargain with God with promises of commitment and sacrifice? How often, once the crisis passes, do we actually follow through? The psalmist committed his life to God using three different images of servitude. The first term, "servant," is the basic word for a bond-slave or personal servant. "Son of Your handmaid" refers to a second category of servitude—inherited through the status of the mother (see Exod. 21:4). While the final phrase points to liberation, "you have loosed my bonds," the psalmist committed to continue to serve out of his love for the Master. "What shall I render to the LORD For all His benefits toward me" (Ps. 116:12)? The answer in Psalm 116 is a life of worship and service to God.

Discipleship's Path (Mark 8:34–37)

Jesus spoke often of the total commitment required by disciples. The gracious gift of God in the death and resurrection of Jesus calls for a radical response by disciples. Jesus' teaching in Mark 8:34–37 comes right on the heels of the pivotal moment of the Gospel. In the very first verse of Mark, we learn the true identity of Jesus. He is "Jesus

Christ, the Son of God" (Mark 1:1). As the Gospel unfolds, everyone in the story is struggling with Jesus' identity. The disciples followed Jesus based on his promise of what he would make them—"fishers of men"—rather than on their clear understanding of Jesus (1:17). Jesus' family thought he had "lost his senses" (3:21). The religious leaders believed he was in league with Satan (3:22). It takes until Mark 8:29 for someone to finally hit on the right answer, as Peter confessed, "You are the Christ." Jesus, however, clarified that confession. Expectations of Jesus' day were that the Christ, or the Messiah, would be a victorious leader in the mold of David who would lead Israel to independence and glory. In verse 29, Jesus described his path leading to rejection, suffering, and death.

In verses 34–37, Jesus shared what this path means for disciples and would-be disciples. These words were spoken not just to the Twelve but to the ever-present, miracle-seeking crowds. The conditional preposition, "if" introduces conditions for discipleship. Our response to God's great gift of Jesus Christ lies in self-denial and taking up the cross. That latter phrase struck their ears differently than it does ours. Looking around my own home, we have crosses on the wall, on jewelry, on t-shirts, on book covers, on dressers, on bookcases, and on bedside tables. From day to day, we might see crosses on bumper stickers, crosses on billboards, crosses tattooed on forearms, giant crosses by the side of the road, and small crosses swinging from mirrors of vehicles. For believers today, the cross may bring up feelings of comfort, solidarity, peace, salvation, or wholeness. I would guess, however, that when Jesus uttered the words, "he must . . . take up his cross," the crowd gasped. In their day, the cross was a horror. It was a demeaning, torturous, and shameful death. About a century before Jesus, the great Roman statesman, Cicero, proclaimed, "What, then, shall I say of crucifixion? It is impossible to find the word for such an abomination. . . . Let the very mention of the cross be far removed not only from a Roman citizen's body, but from his mind, his eyes, his ears."[1] Self-denial and taking up the cross mark the way of discipleship as a path that will not bring personal glory. The path is not for dabblers. This is a way of total commitment, no matter what comes in life.

Verse 35 gives us the most common statement of Jesus' teaching recorded in Scripture. With the *save-lose* and *lose-save* statements, Jesus revealed a deep irony. God has shown us the way by giving to us abundantly, exuberantly, and completely. We gain life by doing the same and giving all to him. Our fallen nature, however, leads us to hoard, cling, and grasp. We are diminished by holding and clinging to "things." The great words of wisdom from Proverbs capture the result well: "There is a way which seems right to a man, But its end is the way of death" (Proverbs 16:25). God has shown us the way. We are to give our whole lives.

A Disciple's Charge (2 Timothy 1:8–12)

In what is perhaps his most personal letter, Paul called Timothy to a response of boldness and sacrifice in following Jesus. Writing from prison, Paul knew that the time for his death had come (2 Timothy 4:6). In this letter he handed the charge and commission to Timothy to carry on God's mission.

In this passage, Paul repeated that foundational gift of God. Our calling as disciples flows from God's calling through the grace of Jesus Christ, "who abolished death and brought life and immortality to light through the gospel" (2 Tim. 1:10). The first response Paul listed to this gift is boldness of testimony: "Do not be ashamed" (1:8). Young Timothy might have doubted where his path would lead, given Paul's imprisonment in Rome. As Jesus said in Mark 8, however, discipleship calls us to follow the path in confident trust, wherever it might lead.

The second response listed by Paul was to "join with me in suffering for the gospel" (1:8). Paul refused to couch discipleship in easy or cheap terms. This is no *soft sell* about the benefits of Christianity for us. One scholar commented, "Any teaching that denies the necessity of suffering is in direct opposition to Paul's gospel, which embraces suffering as a necessary part of the Christian experience."[2] Such an idea is daunting, to be sure. We can share Paul's confidence, however, for God is trustworthy with our whole lives (1:14).

Implications and Actions

The psalmist asked, "What shall I render to the LORD for all His benefits toward me" (Ps. 116:12)? How would you answer that question? The passages in this lesson focus on worship, a life of service to God, self-denial, a willingness to lose our lives for God's sake, boldness in testimony, and a willingness to suffer.

In our culture of religious indifference and tolerance, such commitments might seem quaint or unnecessary. Too often today, the gospel is offered in self-help terms, as something to sooth our guilt or anxieties. The call to complete devotion still sounds, however. God's giving nature still stands, and his is the model we are to follow.

We still have the opportunities to give bold, clear witness to Christ and to make worship an unquestioned, regular part of our lives. We still can respond to God's giving nature with a willingness to give our time, money, work, and relationships to God's service.

THOMAS HELWYS AND RELIGIOUS LIBERTY

While suffering for our faith often seems far from our experience, many of our Baptist forefathers suffered for their boldness of witness to what was right. As Baptists emerged in the early 1600s, one of their distinguishing beliefs was the call for religious liberty. Thomas Helwys was one of these earliest leaders. Along with John Smyth, he founded what many historians believe was the first Baptist church.

Helwys believed strongly in religious liberty. He wrote a letter to King James I and included a copy of his book, *A Short Declaration of the Mistery of Iniquity*. His message to the king included the following comment, "If the Kings people be obedient & true subjects, obeying all humane lawes made by the King, our Lord the King can require no more. For mens religion to God is betwixt God and themselves; the King shall not answer for it, neither may the King be judg betwene God and man."[3] For his boldness, the king threw Helwys into prison, where he died four years later.

REFLECTING ON DISCIPLESHIP

- Take an inventory of a typical week's activities.

- Examine how your priorities line up with your response to God's grace.

- Examine how your spending patterns reflect your discipleship and commitment to God.

- Think about your relationships with friends and family. Find ways either to give witness or to grow together in discipleship.

QUESTIONS

1. Have you ever bargained with God in a time of trouble? Do you carry through with your promises?

2. When was the last time you gave bold witness to or before others?

3. What does self-denial look like in your life?

4. How would you complete the sentence, *Because of what God has done for me, I will . . .?*

NOTES

1. Philip Graham Ryken and James Montgomery Boice, *The Heart of the Cross* (Wheaton, Illinois: Crossway Books, 1999), 120.

2. William D. Mounce, *Pastoral Epistles*, Word Biblical Commentary, Vol. 46 (Nashville, TN: Thomas Nelson Publishers, 2000), 480- 481.

3. Thomas Helwys, *The Mistery of Iniquity, 1612* in H. Leon McBeth, *A Sourcebook for Baptist Heritage* (Nashville, TN: Broadman Press, 1990), 72.

—U N I T   T W O—

Examples That Encourage

Unit two, "Examples That Encourage," contains four lessons based on life in the early church. Each lesson shows how committed believers came to express their faith by courageously living generously and freely.

UNIT TWO. EXAMPLES THAT ENCOURAGE

LESSON FOUR

God's Glad-Hearted People

MAIN IDEA

The Jerusalem church models
the joyous unity in Christ
that leads to generous sharing
of life and possessions

QUESTION TO EXPLORE

What would it take for your
church to be more like the glad-
hearted Jerusalem church?

STUDY AIM

To describe the Jerusalem church's
experience of generous Christian
community and to identify how our
church could grow in such generosity

QUICK READ

As the believers in the Jerusalem
church gave themselves fully to
God, God developed in them
a spirit of Christian unity and
transformed them from owners to
stewards of all their resources.

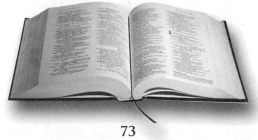

When my husband and I started dating, he wanted me to call him to let him know I got home safely if I was driving home at night. It went pretty smoothly until one night I arrived at my apartment after a late student-ministry event to find the power off. Neither one of us had cell phones, nor would the only phone I had in my apartment work without electricity. I knew he would be worried, but my other option was to drive to a nearby gas station and call him from there. I reasoned that if he knew what was going on he would rather me stay in my locked apartment than venture out again, and so I went to sleep—until I was awakened by a knock at the door. He had driven out to check on me. The next day, he showed up at my apartment with a new flashlight—and a corded phone that would work even in a power failure.

While we laugh about it now, his concern was one of the ways I knew he loved me: he took care of my needs. I tried to take care of his—such as raising his meal quality from bachelor food to things I prepared. We delighted in spending time together—talking, eating, ministering, and worshiping. As we moved toward marriage, we began considering our finances and possessions together. Our mindsets began to shift from *his and hers* to *ours*. We were growing in unity with each other.

I think the early days of the church must have been like those early days when I was falling in love. The first believers were passionate about Jesus and about caring for one another. They were united around their common love for Jesus. Sharing their possessions, time, and energy was only natural. After all, that's what you do when you love someone. Their love and gratitude toward God overflowed into participation in a loving, joyous, and generous community. That's the story we find in Acts 2.

ACTS 2:41–47

41 So then, those who had received his word were baptized; and that day there were added about three thousand souls.

42 They were continually devoting themselves to the apostles' teaching and to fellowship, to the breaking of bread and to prayer.

43 Everyone kept feeling a sense of awe; and many wonders and signs were taking place through the apostles.

44 And all those who had believed were together and had all things in common;

45 and they began selling their property and possessions and were sharing them with all, as anyone might have need.

46 Day by day continuing with one mind in the temple, and breaking bread from house to house, they were taking their meals together with gladness and sincerity of heart,

47 praising God and having favor with all the people. And the Lord was adding to their number day by day those who were being saved.

ACTS 4:32–35

32 And the congregation of those who believed were of one heart and soul; and not one of them claimed that anything belonging to him was his own, but all things were common property to them.

33 And with great power the apostles were giving testimony to the resurrection of the Lord Jesus, and abundant grace was upon them all.

34 For there was not a needy person among them, for all who were owners of land or houses would sell them and bring the proceeds of the sales

35 and lay them at the apostles' feet, and they would be distributed to each as any had need.

A Common Life (Acts 2:41–47)

Fifty days after Jesus ascended into heaven, Jews from all over the world gathered in Jerusalem to celebrate the Feast of Weeks or First Fruits. During the feast on the day of Pentecost, the disciples were gathered together when something extraordinary happened: God sent the Holy Spirit. A sound like a rushing wind filled the room, tongues of fire appeared over the heads of the disciples, and Peter preached his first sermon. All who were assembled, no matter what nation they were from, heard the message in their own language. Some thought the disciples were drunk, but others were amazed. On that day, more than 3,000 people believed and were baptized. The church was born (Acts 2:1–41).

Remember that everything the early Christians experienced was new. No one had developed any church growth models or community profiles. This church wasn't just *First Church Jerusalem*; it was the first church anywhere. All that these early believers had were the words of Jesus, the Old Testament Scriptures, and the indwelling of the Holy Spirit. What they chose to do was to live life together. United around a common Savior, they began to live a common life.

Acts 2:42 says that "they were continually devoting themselves to the apostle's teaching and to fellowship, to the breaking of bread and to prayer."[1] Many have noticed that the activities listed in this verse define the purposes of the church. The "apostles' teaching" would have their accounts of Jesus' life and teachings as the Holy Spirit brought back to their memory all Jesus had said to them (John 14:26). The apostles also would have taught from the Old Testament, showing how the prophecies and stories were fulfilled in the Messiah, Jesus Christ.

"Fellowship" means participation or sharing in common. Together, these early believers would have participated in discussing the apostles' teaching and challenging one another in obedience to Christ. Their sharing of life also extended to a sharing of possessions in order to meet the needs of the community (Acts 2:44–45). We'll look at how they shared in more detail later in the lesson.

"Breaking of bread" probably refers to the sharing of the Lord's Supper as Jesus himself had modeled for them (Matthew 26:20–30). In this act of worship, they remembered Christ's sacrifice for them and gave thanks for what his death had accomplished. At this early stage in the life of the church, they probably took the Lord's Supper as part of a common meal shared in various homes.

These first believers also devoted themselves to prayer. We know that the early church spent much time in prayer, praying both privately and with the gathered church. Some continued the Jewish custom of praying three times a day and going to the temple at the set hours of prayer (Acts 3:1).

Note that they were "continually devoted" to all these things. It wasn't just a passing interest or a brief craze. They didn't settle for simply showing up or warming a pew. They zealously and ardently gave themselves to Bible study, worship, fellowship, and prayer. Their unity flowed from a generous sharing of self. Christ had held nothing back from them, and they held nothing back from one another.

Under the guidance of the Holy Spirit, these early believers gave themselves fully to God and to one another. Amazing things happened. "Everyone kept feeling a sense of awe, and many wonders and signs were taking place through the apostles" (2:43). I think of awe as a sense of wonder mixed with holy fear. God was doing something new among them. Just as God had marked the birth of the nation of Israel with signs and wonders (Deuteronomy 4:34; 26:8), God marked the birth of the church with many miracles done through the apostles.

The new believers generously shared their possessions, but they also generously shared their time. "Day by day, as they spent much time together in the temple, they broke bread at home and ate their food with glad and generous hearts" (Acts 2:46, New Revised Standard Version). Our busy lives often lead us to be stingy with our time, but true community cannot be born in only a couple of hours on Sunday morning. Christians in the Jerusalem church formed community by daily spending time together, both in worship and in each other's homes. Forming community means that we have to let down our barriers and truly become a part of one another's lives.

As the first church began to grow in unity among believers and with Christ, people began to notice. The result was an almost magnetic attraction. They had "favor with all the people. And the Lord was adding to their number day by day those who were being saved" (2:47, NASB). Today, many people have negative opinions of church. Some of them are justified. But when God's people get it right, when we freely give ourselves to God and to one another, people still take notice. What would it look like for your church to live a common life?

A Common Heart (Acts 4:32–35)

The first believers' common life led them to develop a common heart. They were characterized by a great sense of unity. They were "of one heart and soul" (4:32). This unity of heart and soul overflowed into a generous sharing of possessions. The first church acted like a family, giving graciously to meet the needs of all family members without expectation of return.

Giving without expecting anything in return would have been a surprising concept in the New Testament world. In Greco-Roman culture, almost any exchange of property or possession included some type of reciprocity. The culture was built around the idea of *patronage*, where those in power cultivated *clients* who were bound to them by their *friendship. Patrons* earned their client's *friendship* by giving favors or privileges. In exchange, patrons received loyalty, honor, and power.

The idea of patronage is entirely absent in the early church. Those who gave were motivated not by a desire to curry favor, but out of a conviction that none among them should be in need (Deut. 15:4). They were not content just to fellowship in worship; they regarded others' needs as their own. Giving without expectation of return took the element of power out of the relationship. Poor and rich alike related as equals in the church, brothers and sisters in Christ (Galatians 3:28). That the apostles distributed funds as there was need further broke down the traditional power structures. Since the funds were distributed through the apostles, recipients wouldn't know the specific donor of the gift. This made it impossible for patrons to cultivate clients by giving through the church.

Sometimes people make the mistake of thinking that early believers sold everything they owned when they joined the community, as if they were joining some type of commune. This was not the case. They continued to meet from "house to house" (Acts 2:46), and we see later in Acts that Mary, mother of John Mark, still lived in her own home (12:12). Instead, it seems that those who had an abundance voluntarily sold property in order to use their resources to meet the needs of the community. Property was not controlled by the community, and giving was voluntary (5:4).

Although believers did not give up all their possessions, we should not underestimate the radical shift in how they viewed their possessions. Their understanding of their wealth shifted from *owner* to *steward*. They recognized that their possessions were not meant for stockpiling wealth, but were God-given resources meant for enabling the work of God's kingdom. That work included meeting the needs of this new family of faith. As members of a family, they stopped seeing their possessions as *mine* but began to call them *ours*.

Ideas and Implications

Every once in a while I run into someone who says something along the lines of how tithing is an Old Testament concept. In a sense, they're right, for the New Testament idea goes far beyond only giving ten percent. In fact, the New Testament idea is that everything we have belongs to God. Our money, time, and talents all belong to him. In that sense, tithing is the bare minimum God requires of us.

The Jerusalem church understood that. They didn't commit only to agreeing around the same ideas or seeing one another on Sunday morning and Wednesday nights. They experienced community on an intimate level. They became part of one another's lives as they worshiped, fellowshipped, learned, and prayed together on a daily basis. Out of that unity, they came to regard one another's needs as their own.

Are we willing to undergo a similar transformation? We live in a culture that prizes materialism, individualism, and consumption. We excel at compartmentalizing our lives, time, and wealth. Living in community means that we must not settle for occupying a common space; we must seek to live a common life. We must generously give of our time, talents, and possessions to meet the needs around us. What would you have to change to experience this kind of community?

FELLOWSHIP IN THE NEW TESTAMENT

The Greek word for fellowship, *koinonia*, carries the idea of participation. Usually it doesn't refer to an abstract concept but to an active and personal partnership. We may have co-opted the term to refer to a potluck meal or pie social, but in the New Testament it is used with a sense of sharing and self-sacrifice. In Acts this is demonstrated in the generous sharing of possessions among believers. Paul also used it in his letters to describe the actions of Gentile believers who gave to meet the needs of Jewish Christians in Jerusalem.

We can experience fellowship in negative ways when we participate in another's sins (1 Timothy 5:22; 2 John 11). But true believers participate in the sufferings of Christ and in the suffering of fellow Christians (Philippians 3:10; Hebrews 10:33). Through the fellowship of the Holy Spirit, we also become partakers of the divine nature (2 Peter 1:4) and the glory of Christ's coming kingdom (1 Peter 5:1).

CASE STUDY

A teenage girl in your youth group has been late to school every day this week. You find out that her mother is seriously ill. The girl has essentially become responsible for parenting her younger brother and sister, including getting them dressed and to school on time each day.

What are some practical ways your church could help meet needs in this situation?

QUESTIONS

1. How many hours did you spend last week on each of the following activities: exercise, entertainment, work, sleep, time with family, eating, driving, church, Bible study, and prayer? How does where you spend your time reflect what you are most devoted to?

2. How does your church fulfill the purposes of discipleship, worship, fellowship, and prayer?

3. In what ways do you see yourself as owner of your possessions? as steward?

4. What are some ways your church is involved practically in meeting needs? What are some ways you can grow in this area?

5. How have you seen your church family demonstrate unity?

NOTES ————————————————————————————

1. Unless otherwise indicated, all Scripture quotations in lessons 1–7 and the introductions to units 1 and 2 are taken from the 1995 update of the New American Standard Bible®.

FOCAL TEXT
Acts 4:36–37; 11:19–26;
15:36–40

BACKGROUND
Acts 4:32–37; 9:26–27;
11:19–26; 13:2–3;
14:8–12; 15:1–40

LESSON FIVE

Always Encouraging

MAIN IDEA

Barnabas models the generosity of life that brings encouragement to others and is to characterize followers of Jesus.

QUESTION TO EXPLORE

Who are the people you recall or most hope to see when you need encouragement?

STUDY AIM

To identify ways in which Barnabas modeled encouragement and to measure my life by these qualities

QUICK READ

Like Barnabas, we can model encouragement by words and actions to welcome people into the family of faith and help them discover their kingdom potential.

In his book *Remember Why You Play*, sportswriter David Thomas tells the story of a game between two unlikely opponents. In November 2008, the Faith Christian Lions of Grapevine, Texas, had clinched a playoff berth before the last game of the season. The game should have been meaningless. Their opponent, the Gainesville State Tornadoes, was a team from a maximum-security correctional facility. The Tornadoes had lost eight games straight and had scored only two touchdowns all season. They traveled for every game under armed guard and had no home field and few fans. Even playing backups and junior varsity players, the Lions should have easily run away with the game.

However, Lions' Head Coach Kris Hogan saw an opportunity to encourage the Gainesville students. Hogan sent out a message to the Faith Christian parents asking for them to make the Gainesville Tornadoes their team for the night. When the Tornadoes started to take the field, they were in for the shock of their lives.

As the Tornadoes took the field, they were greeted by a line of Faith fans forming a spirit line for the Tornadoes. Faith fans filled the visitors' bleachers, armed with Tornadoes team rosters. Faith's junior varsity cheerleaders led the crowds in cheering for the Tornadoes. When the team began to hear the crowd yelling their names, a few players first thought there must be someone on the Lions' team with the same name. They soon realized the cheers were for them.

Faith won 33–14, but the unprecedented support made it feel like a Tornadoes' victory. At the end of the night, the Tornadoes' quarterback led the crowd in a simple prayer: "Lord, I don't know how this happened so I don't know how to say thank you, but I never would have known there were so many people in the world that cared about us."[1]

Somehow that game changed the culture of the school. The Gainesville players returned home with their heads held high. Students began looking for ways to serve others. Behavioral offenses decreased. The Gainesville staff was re-energized. As media attention grew, outside support for the Gainesville students also increased. Students began to believe that there were people out there who would give them a second chance and that despite their mistakes of the past, they could still re-enter the world and make a positive impact. Encouragement is powerful.

ACTS 4:36–37

[36] Now Joseph, a Levite of Cyprian birth, who was also called Barnabas by the apostles (which translated means Son of Encouragement),

[37] and who owned a tract of land, sold it and brought the money and laid it at the apostles' feet.

ACTS 11:19–26

19 So then those who were scattered because of the persecution that occurred in connection with Stephen made their way to Phoenicia and Cyprus and Antioch, speaking the word to no one except to Jews alone.

20 But there were some of them, men of Cyprus and Cyrene, who came to Antioch and *began* speaking to the Greeks also, preaching the Lord Jesus.

21 And the hand of the Lord was with them, and a large number who believed turned to the Lord.

22 The news about them reached the ears of the church at Jerusalem, and they sent Barnabas off to Antioch.

23 Then when he arrived and witnessed the grace of God, he rejoiced and began to encourage them all with resolute heart to remain true to the Lord;

24 for he was a good man, and full of the Holy Spirit and of faith. And considerable numbers were brought to the Lord.

25 And he left for Tarsus to look for Saul;

26 and when he had found him, he brought him to Antioch. And for an entire year they met with the church and taught considerable numbers; and the disciples were first called Christians in Antioch.

ACTS 15:36–40

[36] After some days Paul said to Barnabas, "Let us return and visit the brethren in every city in which we proclaimed the word of the Lord, and see how they are."

[37] Barnabas wanted to take John, called Mark, along with them also.

[38] But Paul kept insisting that they should not take him along who had deserted them in Pamphylia and had not gone with them to the work.

[39] And there occurred such a sharp disagreement that they separated from one another, and Barnabas took Mark with him and sailed away to Cyprus.

[40] But Paul chose Silas and left, being committed by the brethren to the grace of the Lord.

Generous in Giving (Acts 4:36–37)

In lesson four, we looked at how the early church generously shared their possessions with one another to meet the needs of the community. In Acts 4:36, Luke gave an example of one such person: Joseph, better known as Barnabas, "son of encouragement."

We learn a few things about Barnabas from these verses. First, Barnabas was a model of generosity. He sold some of his property and brought the proceeds to the apostles so that they might distribute them to those in need.

Barnabas served as an example to the early church—and to us—of generous giving.

Barnabas's nickname, from the Aramaic expression *bar nabi*, which literally means *son of a prophet*, also tells us something about his nature. It may have been a reference to his teaching role in the early church (Acts 11:23; 13:1). Yet it also tells us something about his personality. Barnabas was a person who saw the potential in others and encouraged them to grow in their faithfulness and devotion to the Lord.

A Generous Welcome (Acts 11:19–26)

When you're walking into an unfamiliar situation, it always feels good to see someone you know. It's welcoming to have someone there who knows you and can draw you into the group. That's a little of what's going on in this passage: new Gentile believers needed someone to fully welcome them into what had been a predominantly Jewish church.

After Stephen, one of the early church leaders, was martyred, a great persecution broke out against the Jerusalem church (7:54—8:1). Many believers fled Jerusalem and spread the gospel to fellow Jews along the way. Some of those scattered believers came to Antioch and began to proclaim the gospel to Gentiles, or non-Jews. These first converts may have been *God-fearers* such as Cornelius.

God-fearers were Gentiles who had embraced the God of Israel (10:1–2) but chose not to be circumcised to become Jews.

When the news reached Jerusalem, the church sent Barnabas to Antioch to investigate the situation. It may have been that the apostles chose Barnabas because he, like some of the original missionaries, was from Cyprus. Certainly Barnabas was also chosen because of his character. Barnabas is the only man in the Book of Acts called "good" (11:24). Luke also described him as "full of the Holy Spirit and of faith."

Think about the people in your community whom you would consider least likely to ever receive the gospel. Now imagine that one morning you walked into church and saw them all lining the back row. Would you wonder why they were there? Would you think that it was about time they got their lives straight? Would you hope the preacher had a fire and brimstone sermon that morning?

Barnabas did none of those things. He looked at this group of new believers and saw God's grace at work. He rejoiced to see what God was doing among them. He encouraged them all with "resolute heart to remain true to the Lord" (11:23). Under his teaching great numbers of people came to know the Lord.

Before long, Barnabas needed help. He went to Tarsus to look for Saul. This also tells us something about Barnabas—where others might have seen the past, Barnabas saw potential. It wasn't all that long before that

Saul had been a persecutor of the church (8:1; 9:1–2). After his dramatic conversion as he travelled to Damascus, Barnabas brought him to the apostles and vouched for the sincerity of his conversion (9:27–28). Death threats on his life forced Saul back to Tarsus, where he remained for some time. But now Barnabas needed him. Saul had been trained as a rabbi and was highly competent in understanding the Scriptures. He also spoke Greek and was an excellent debater. Most importantly, God had commissioned Saul to preach Christ to the Gentiles (9:15–16). Barnabas went to Tarsus to look for Saul and brought Saul back to Antioch. Little did Barnabas know that this one act of encouragement would change the history of the church. By the end of Saul's life—better known to us as Paul—he would have authored thirteen books of the New Testament and preached the gospel in what is now Israel, Lebanon, Turkey, Syria, Greece, Italy, Crete, and perhaps even Spain.

Barnabas and Saul returned to Antioch and taught the church there. Perhaps because of the influx of Gentiles into the church, the community began to recognize the church as something more than another Jewish sect. In Antioch, the disciples were first called "Christians" (literally *little Christs*; 11:26).

Generous in Giving Second Chances (Acts 15:36–40)

One thing that stood out about the game between Faith Christian and Gainesville State is how much it meant to the Gainesville kids to know someone was willing to give them a second chance. In some ways, for us to say that God can give a kid from reform school a second chance is easy. After all, God forgives and restores. It's much harder to give someone a second chance when they've personally wronged you.

That's the problem that confronted Paul and Barnabas in Acts 15. On their first missionary journey, they took John Mark, Barnabas's cousin, with them as their helper (13:5). John Mark made it through the first leg of the journey before heading back home to Jerusalem (13:13). The Bible doesn't give us the reason for his departure, but Paul plainly regarded it as desertion (15:38).

John Mark's early departure from the mission set the stage for later conflict between Paul and Barnabas. Paul later wanted to return to the churches they had founded on their first trip to see how the new congregations were faring. Barnabas agreed, but wanted to take John Mark along with them. Paul did not want to take along someone who had previously deserted them, and a "sharp disagreement" rose up between them (13:37–39).

"Sharp disagreement" is a bit of an understatement. The Greek word used here is the root from which we get the English word *paroxysm*, as in *paroxysm of rage*. It carries with it the picture of someone red-faced, literally shaking with anger. And there is a sense—as sometimes happens in church conflicts—in which Paul and Barnabas were both correct. Paul needed reliable people with him on his missionary journeys, people he knew he could count on if, for example, he had to face an angry mob (14:4–5).

As he had with Paul, Barnabas saw potential instead of the past failure. Barnabas was willing to give John Mark a chance to redeem his past and prove himself faithful. Unable to come to agreement, Barnabas and Paul parted. Paul took Silas and returned to visit the churches of Galatia. Barnabas took John Mark and went to Cyprus (15:38–40).

Thankfully, that's not the end of the story. This is the last time Barnabas is mentioned in Scripture, but it's not the last we hear of John Mark. Barnabas's encouragement of and investment in John Mark bore fruit. About twelve years later, Paul was writing letters from a Roman prison. John Mark, who had previously *deserted* Paul, was with him and sent greetings to the churches to which Paul wrote (Colossians 4:10; Philemon 24). Still later, at the close of Paul's life, he asked Timothy to bring John Mark to him, for "he is useful to me for service" (2 Timothy 4:11). Tradition tells us that John Mark wrote the Gospel of Mark. Encouragement is powerful.

Implications and Actions

Barnabas saw the world differently than others did. Where some might have seen the Gentile converts in Antioch as unwelcome outsiders, Barnabas saw God's grace at work. When seeing a young man who had failed greatly, Barnabas saw his potential although others might have seen only his past. In both cases, Barnabas used his gift of encouragement to spur others on to faithfulness and growth in Christ. Antioch became a missional, sending church. John Mark became an evangelist.

We have that same opportunity as Barnabas to encourage by example, words, and actions. But we must learn to view the world differently. When the person we think will never darken the doors of the church does, do we see God's grace at work in them? When we look at people who once had a past, are we willing to see their future potential? Who is there in your life that needs to be fully welcomed into the family of faith? Who needs to be offered a second chance? Encouragement is powerful. Are you willing to be Barnabas to someone today?

R. C. BUCKNER: FATHER OF BAPTIST BENEVOLENCE

Prior to R. C. Buckner's arrival in Texas after the Civil War, Texas Baptists did not have any organized way of addressing social needs such as child care or elder care. Buckner saw the need and went to work. In 1879, Buckner founded the Buckner Baptist Children's Home with $2,000 donated by Texas Baptists. Buckner himself guaranteed a large portion of the money. The Children's Home became a point of unity for Texas Baptists. In addition to financial gifts, Texas Baptists supported the home by sending lumber, fabric, cows, pigs, eggs, clothing, and baked goods.

Although he is known best for his founding of the children's home, Buckner also helped guide Texas Baptists in supporting elder care, hospitals, theological education for women, and prison ministry. Guided by their convictions that personal faith was demonstrated in charitable action, under Buckner's leadership, Texas Baptists began to identify societal needs and worked to impact them.[2]

Ways to Encourage

- Provide a scholarship for a seminary student or funds for a mission trip.

- Write a note to someone going through a difficult time.

- Carry a meal to a family coping with illness.

- Give a caregiver an afternoon break.

- Welcome a visitor to your church.

- Help someone find a new opportunity for ministry.

QUESTIONS

1. Think of someone who has been an encouragement to you. How did that encouragement affect you?

2. How can we learn to look at people and see their potential rather than their past?

3. What group in your community might need the encouragement of a generous welcome into the family of faith? How could you reach out to them?

4. When have you needed a second chance? How could you extend that same opportunity to others?

NOTES

1. David Thomas, *Remember Why You Play* (Carol Stream: Thomas Nelson, 2010), 231.

2. Karen O'Dell Bullock, *The Life and Contributions of Robert Cooke Buckner: Progenitor of Organized Social Christianity among Texas Baptists, 1860–1919*, Doctoral Dissertation, Southwestern Baptist Theological Seminary, 1991.

FOCAL TEXT

1 Corinthians 16:1–4;
2 Corinthians
8:1–15; 9:6–15

BACKGROUND

Acts 24:17;
Romans 15:25–29;
1 Corinthians 16:1–4;
2 Corinthians 8—9;
Galatians 2:10

LESSON SIX

Giving Themselves First

MAIN IDEA

The collection for the saints models generosity in the giving of material possessions in response to the example of Christ and the needs of others.

QUESTIONS TO EXPLORE

Why give?

STUDY AIM

To identify motivations for giving material possessions and to decide how I will respond to these motivations

QUICK READ

Christ's generosity toward us should stimulate our generous response toward the needs of others.

George W. Truett (1867–1944), the legendary Baptist preacher, pastor, and leader,[1] often spent his summers in West Texas preaching to the Paisano cowboy camp. He saw hundreds of the cowboys *come under to the Master,* the words they used to refer to conversion.

As Truett preached the gospel, he sought to cultivate a sense of Christian stewardship in his listeners. One night a ranch owner drew Truett aside after the service and asked Truett to walk with him a while. Truett could see the man was struggling with emotion. When the rancher finally was able to speak, he asked Truett if he would pray a dedicatory prayer for him. The rancher said that until that morning he had not realized that all his cattle were not really his own but the Lord's. He wanted to dedicate them to God and continue as an administrator of God's estate. Truett did as he was asked. After he prayed, the man also prayed, dedicating his wayward son to the Lord. That evening, the son stood up fifteen minutes into the sermon and declared that he could not wait until the sermon was over to come to the Lord.

When we give ourselves to God, we give all we have to God. Like Truett's cowboy friend, we are to see ourselves as administrators of God's estate rather than owners of our own property. Our growing in understanding of the generous grace God has given us should prompt us to be generous toward others. The passages for study in this lesson show us that Paul also taught his converts about Christian stewardship.[2]

1 CORINTHIANS 16:1–4

1 Now concerning the collection for the saints, as I directed the churches of Galatia, so do you also.

2 On the first day of every week each one of you is to put aside and save, as he may prosper, so that no collections be made when I come.

3 When I arrive, whomever you may approve, I will send them with letters to carry your gift to Jerusalem;

4 and if it is fitting for me to go also, they will go with me.

2 CORINTHIANS 8:1–15

1 Now, brethren, we wish to make known to you the grace of God which has been given in the churches of Macedonia,

2 that in a great ordeal of affliction their abundance of joy and their deep poverty overflowed in the wealth of their liberality.

3 For I testify that according to their ability, and beyond their ability, they gave of their own accord,

4 begging us with much urging for the favor of participation in the support of the saints,

5 and this, not as we had expected, but they first gave themselves to the Lord and to us by the will of God.

6 So we urged Titus that as he had previously made a beginning, so he would also complete in you this gracious work as well.

7 But just as you abound in everything, in faith and utterance and knowledge and in all earnestness and in the love we inspired in you, see that you abound in this gracious work also.

8 I am not speaking this as a command, but as proving through the earnestness of others the sincerity of your love also.

9 For you know the grace of our Lord Jesus Christ, that though He was rich, yet for your sake He became poor, so that you through His poverty might become rich.

10 I give my opinion in this matter, for this is to your advantage, who were the first to begin a year ago not only to do this, but also to desire to do it.

11 But now finish doing it also, so that just as there was the readiness to desire it, so there may be also the completion of it by your ability.

12 For if the readiness is present, it is acceptable according to what a person has, not according to what he does not have.

13 For this is not for the ease of others and for your affliction, but by way of equality—

14 at this present time your abundance being a supply for their need, so that their abundance also may become a supply for your need, that there may be equality;

15 as it is written, "HE WHO gathered MUCH DID NOT HAVE TOO MUCH, AND HE WHO gathered LITTLE HAD NO LACK."

2 CORINTHIANS 9:6–15

⁶ Now this I say, he who sows sparingly will also reap sparingly, and he who sows bountifully will also reap bountifully.

⁷ Each one must do just as he has purposed in his heart, not grudgingly or under compulsion, for God loves a cheerful giver.

⁸ And God is able to make all grace abound to you, so that always having all sufficiency in everything, you may have an abundance for every good deed;

⁹ as it is written,

"HE SCATTERED ABROAD, HE GAVE TO THE POOR,

HIS RIGHTEOUSNESS ENDURES FOREVER."

¹⁰ Now He who supplies seed to the sower and bread for food will supply and multiply your seed for sowing and increase the harvest of your righteousness;

¹¹ you will be enriched in everything for all liberality, which through us is producing thanksgiving to God.

¹² For the ministry of this service is not only fully supplying the needs of the saints, but is also overflowing through many thanksgivings to God.

¹³ Because of the proof given by this ministry, they will glorify God for your obedience to your confession of the gospel of Christ and for the liberality of your contribution to them and to all,

¹⁴ while they also, by prayer on your behalf, yearn for you because of the surpassing grace of God in you.

¹⁵ Thanks be to God for His indescribable gift!

A Collection for the Saints (1 Corinthians 16:1–4)

Paul responded in 1 Corinthians to several questions raised by the Corinthian church in a previous letter to the apostle. One of those questions had to do with the "collection for the saints" (1 Corinthians 16:1).

During what is known as the "Jerusalem Council," the church determined that Gentile converts would not have to first become Jews—including being circumcised—before following Christ (Acts 15:1–29). The council commissioned Paul and Barnabas to preach to the Gentiles, but asked Paul to "remember the poor" (Galatians 2:10). Paul asked the Gentile churches to take up an offering for the relief of the poor in Jerusalem. In lesson four, we saw how the first believers expressed their unity by sharing possessions to meet needs. Paul saw the offering as an expression of unity between the Jewish and Gentile churches in that same spirit. The Gentiles would share material possessions with the Jewish people who had shared their spiritual inheritance with them (Romans 15:26–28).

In 1 Corinthians 16, Paul gave simple instructions for how the church was to collect the offering. On the first day of the week, each person was to set aside a portion of his or her income so that it would be ready when Paul came to collect it and send it on to Jerusalem. He also noted that the Corinthians should choose one of their own members to carry the money to Jerusalem. That way the church could be assured that the funds would be directed as they had intended and not appropriated as *overhead* by Paul or his companions. In this particular passage, there is no suggestion of a tithe or giving in proportion to one's income; Paul simply advised that each person give "as he may prosper" (1 Cor. 16:2). In other words, as God allows each one to prosper, he or she should set aside some of whatever abundance God might provide that week. The plan was striking in its simplicity. Paul made no efforts at manipulation, no emotional appeals, and no promises of a spiritual jackpot. He simply laid out a matter-of-fact plan for the church to follow.

Complete What You Have Begun (2 Corinthians 8:1–15)

I am always amazed by the faithful giving of some of the least wealthy church members. When I was teaching youth Sunday School, one Christmas our class discussed the Lottie Moon Christmas Offering for International Missions. The class decided to try to fill a large jar with change over the next several weeks for their offering. The next Sunday I watched as a young woman came in and emptied a plastic sandwich bag filled with change into the jar. I knew that she was from a home where resources were scarce, and so I asked her about her gift. She told me that the bag contained five dollars of change. She had been saving it for something she wanted, but decided to give it to the Lottie Moon Offering instead. Her sacrificial example challenged me. My husband and I had already decided on how much we would give, but I couldn't say that I had really given up something I wanted in order to give. I've often thought the Lord must have done something special with those five dollars.

The young woman's spirit is like the spirit behind Paul's words to the Corinthians in 2 Corinthians 8. Corinth was a wealthy city. The churches of Macedonia were much poorer, and Paul at first had not thought to include them in the collection so as not to further stress their already meager resources. Yet when the Macedonian churches learned of the plan they begged for the privilege of sharing in the collection. Overwhelmed with gratitude at what Christ had done for them, the Macedonian churches generously shared out of what they had.

Paul challenged the Corinthians to follow the example of the Macedonians by completing what they had begun. He further challenged them to follow the example of Christ who "though He was rich, yet for your sake He became poor, so that you through His poverty might become rich" (2 Corinthians 8:9). Jesus willingly laid aside his glory to take on human frailty so that through his sacrifice we could share in his glory. If Christ was so generous with us, how should we reflect that generosity to others?

Paul further stressed that his goal was not to impoverish the Corinthians in order to help those in Jerusalem, but to bring equality (2 Cor. 8:13–15). At this time, the abundance of the Corinthians could be used to help the Jerusalem church, but perhaps later their abundance might supply the Corinthians' need.

Even in the midst of a recession in recent years, America remains a wealthy nation. The World Bank estimates that half of the world's population exists on less than two dollars a day. Some experts estimate that Americans spend as much as $21 billion a year on bottled water, and yet a billion of the world's most vulnerable people lack access to clean drinking water. According to the World Food Program, there is enough food in the world to provide adequate nutrition for every person alive today. Yet, while America wastes nearly half its food each year, seventy per cent of childhood deaths worldwide are due to malnutrition or preventable diseases. God has given us abundance. How have we used it?[3]

God Loves a Cheerful Giver
(2 Corinthians 9:6–15)

It's been said that if we look at the bottom line of our budgets, there are two things we will never do: tithe—and have children. My husband and I have done both, and we have seen God provide for us in amazing ways. After our third child was born, we were juggling our budget trying to figure out how to contribute to a special offering at our church and cover some extra expenses. We got an unexpected check in the mail—a refund from the hospital that more than covered our needs and allowed us to contribute the amount to the offering we had planned to give.

One of the blessings of giving is that we get to see God's provision for us. When God multiplies our harvest, it's not in the sense of a vending machine theology in which we put five dollars in the offering plate and expect to get fifty back next week. Rather, God, who knows our needs, provides us with "an abundance for every good deed" (9:8). God multiplies our seed not for hoarding, but for sowing so that God may use it to bring the harvest. As God's abundant grace overflows toward us, we should overflow in generous grace toward others.

Another blessing of giving is that it brings glory to God. In our giving, we express thanksgiving for all that God has given us. Our giving provides for the needs of others. Those who receive thank God for his provision to them. God is also glorified in that sharing of our resources demonstrates that our lives have been changed. Only God could transform our selfishness into generosity toward others.

Finally, giving produces unity in the church. Paul described how the Jerusalem church would pray for and "yearn" for the Corinthians as they saw God's grace at work through the Corinthians' generosity (9:14). This was what Paul hoped for—that the offering would produce unity between Jews and Gentiles, thus extending globally the unity that the church had begun in Acts. When we give to help others around the world, we claim them as brothers and sisters in Christ, members of the family of God. God is still glorified in our giving.

Implications and Actions

Considering the world's needs can be overwhelming. We are confronted with them every day. Literacy, poverty, immigration, persecution, famine, war, people without access to the gospel—when we see all the needs around us it is easy to feel that anything we could do is too small to make a difference. Overwhelmed, we sometimes shut down.

Perhaps we ask the wrong questions. We ask, *What can I afford to give?* or *How can my little gift matter?* Instead, we should ask ourselves what we would be willing to give to see. What would you give to see? Do you want to see Bibles translated in every language? churches planted among unreached people groups? wells dug? food provided? people treated for AIDS, sexual slaves freed, orphans given homes? What would you give to see these things become reality?

God has given the church the resources needed to do his work. But God-sized tasks require God-sized resources. We must begin to see ourselves as stewards rather than as owners of what God provides. As we do so, we respond to God's generous grace by displaying generosity toward others. In the process, God is glorified.

LOTTIE MOON (1840–1912)

Although born into a strong Christian home, Charlotte "Lottie" Diggs Moon wanted nothing to do with religion until she accepted Christ at age sixteen. A brilliant student who had an aptitude for languages, Lottie was called to missions in February 1873 and appointed to China in July of that year.

In China, Lottie distributed gospel tracts and sometimes stood in the back of a rickshaw so that the crowds could hear her as she shared the good news of Jesus Christ. When she made her infrequent trips stateside, Lottie's presentations helped spark missionary interest among Baptists.

In 1887 Lottie suggested to Baptist women that they observe a week of prayer before Christmas and collect a missions offering. She noted that the time when we celebrate God's gift of Jesus Christ is an appropriate time for us to share a portion of our abundance in order to spread the good news to all the earth. The offering became an annual event, and the Lottie Moon Christmas Offering was named in her honor after her death.[4]

A WEEK OF GIVING

Day 1: Give a nickel for every t-shirt you have in your closet.

Day 2: Give $1 for every Bible you have in your home.

Day 3: Give 25 cents for every glass of water you drink.

Day 4: Give $5 if you have a roof over your head.

Day 5: Give 10 cents every time you use your phone today.

Day 6: Give 25 cents for every hour of television you watch this week.

Day 7: Give 50 cents for every meal you eat today.

Consider giving this offering to the World Hunger Offering or your local food bank.

QUESTIONS

1. Paul used the Macedonians' generosity in spite of their poverty to encourage the wealthier Corinthian church to give. What examples challenge you in your giving?

2. How should thanksgiving for God's generosity toward us impact our view of our possessions?

3. What are some of the blessings of giving? How have you seen those demonstrated in your life?

4. When have you seen God provide an abundance so that his work could be completed?

5. What needs are on your heart that you want to see fulfilled? What would you be willing to give to make those dreams reality?

NOTES

1. See http://www.sbhla.org/bio_gtruett.htm. Accessed 1/6/2012.

2. Powhatan W. James, *George W. Truett: A Biography* (Nashville: Broadman Press, 1939), 111–114.

3. Christian Life Commission, "Hunger Statistics," Internet, available from http://www.bgct.org/texasbaptists/Page.aspx?pid=6819, accessed 11/5/2011; Jeff Harrison, "Nation Wastes Nearly Half Its Food," *UA News*, Internet, available from http://uanews.org/node/10448, accessed 11/6/2011.

4. H. Leon MacBeth, *The Baptist Heritage* (Nashville: Broadman Press, 1987), 416–419.

LESSON SEVEN

More Blessed to Give

MAIN IDEA

Paul's life and ministry model
the importance of generosity
in the Christian life.

QUESTION TO EXPLORE

How is it more blessed to
give than to receive?

STUDY AIM

To describe the ways in which Paul
put into practice Jesus' teaching
about giving being more blessed
than receiving and to describe how
I could live out this statement

QUICK READ

In his ministry at Ephesus, Paul's
proclamation of the gospel,
generous labor, and willingness
to obey at all costs demonstrates
Jesus' teaching that it is more
blessed to give than to receive.

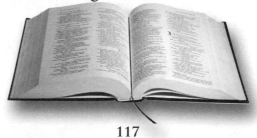

Recently our church hosted the baccalaureate service for our high school seniors. One of our church members, a high school teacher, was asked to give the keynote address. We live in a small school district, and so she was able to call each senior by name. During her speech, she named each one of them and shared a memory from their time in her class. She gave each of them a personal challenge she hoped they would carry with them as they graduated and began a new phase of life. Because she knew and loved them, she was able to address them personally and meaningfully.

The last few months of high school are poignant for parents, teachers, and students. Students know that they will never be gathered together with their friends in exactly the same way again. Parents know that their children will soon be entering adult life and may wonder whether they have instilled in them all they need to know. Teachers know they have finished their role as instructor and prepare to say goodbye to students they have invested in and cared for.

Paul's speech to the Ephesian elders in Acts 20 is a sort of graduation address. Acts 20 records Paul's farewell speech as he left Asia for Jerusalem, never again to return. Of all his speeches, this one sounds the most like Paul's letters. It rings with his love for the church and the poignancy of knowing that he would not return.

ACTS 20:17–35

17 From Miletus he sent to Ephesus and called to him the elders of the church.

18 And when they had come to him, he said to them,

"You yourselves know, from the first day that I set foot in Asia, how I was with you the whole time,

19 serving the Lord with all humility and with tears and with trials which came upon me through the plots of the Jews;

20 how I did not shrink from declaring to you anything that was profitable, and teaching you publicly and from house to house,

21 solemnly testifying to both Jews and Greeks of repentance toward God and faith in our Lord Jesus Christ.

22 "And now, behold, bound by the Spirit, I am on my way to Jerusalem, not knowing what will happen to me there,

23 except that the Holy Spirit solemnly testifies to me in every city, saying that bonds and afflictions await me.

24 "But I do not consider my life of any account as dear to myself, so that I may finish my course and the ministry which I received from the Lord Jesus, to testify solemnly of the gospel of the grace of God.

25 "And now, behold, I know that all of you, among whom I went about preaching the kingdom, will no longer see my face.

26 "Therefore, I testify to you this day that I am innocent of the blood of all men.

27 "For I did not shrink from declaring to you the whole purpose of God.

28 "Be on guard for yourselves and for all the flock, among which the Holy Spirit has made you overseers, to shepherd the church of God which He purchased with His own blood.

29 "I know that after my departure savage wolves will come in among you, not sparing the flock;

30 and from among your own selves men will arise, speaking perverse things, to draw away the disciples after them.

31 "Therefore be on the alert, remembering that night and day for a period of three years I did not cease to admonish each one with tears.

32 "And now I commend you to God and to the word of His grace, which is able to build you up and to give you the inheritance among all those who are sanctified.

33 "I have coveted no one's silver or gold or clothes.

34 "You yourselves know that these hands ministered to my own needs and to the men who were with me.

35 "In everything I showed you that by working hard in this manner you must help the weak and remember the words of the Lord Jesus, that He Himself said, 'It is more blessed to give than to receive.'"

Finishing the Course (Acts 20:17–24)

At the end of Paul's third missionary journey, he headed to Jerusalem to take the offering for the saints that had been contributed by the Gentile churches (see lesson 6). Paul was hoping to be in Jerusalem in time for Pentecost and was somewhat pressed for time, and so he did not want to go into Ephesus lest he be delayed. He asked the elders, or leaders, of the church, to meet him in Miletus so that he might say farewell (Acts 20:16).

This passage makes clear the depth of Paul's love for his churches. Paul had served among them "with all humility and with tears," even though humility was not a quality prized in the ancient world (20:19). Paul had stayed in Ephesus three years—longer than he stayed in any other place during his missionary journeys—and he had faced notable opposition during his stay there. As was his customary practice, Paul began by preaching in the synagogue. He preached there until Jewish opposition grew so intense that he was forced to move to another location (19:8–10). Paul also sparked a riot led by silversmiths who made idols of the goddess Artemis. Apparently Paul's message had drawn so many converts that their business was being negatively impacted, and the silversmiths wanted to sway public opinion (19:23–29). Despite the opposition, Paul did not shrink back from proclaiming to both Jews and Gentiles the truth "of repentance toward God and faith toward our Lord Jesus" (20:21).

Now, led by or "captive" to the Holy Spirit, Paul was on his way to Jerusalem. He knew that he had to go; and yet God had also revealed to him that persecution and imprisonment lay ahead (21:10–11). Paul knew his life might be at risk if he returned to Jerusalem, but his life was less important to him than finishing the task God had entrusted to him, testifying "solemnly to the gospel of the grace of God" (20:24). Paul never forgot the generosity of God's grace to him, the "foremost" of sinners (1 Timothy 1:15). His gratitude to God overflowed into full-hearted devotion and service to the gospel of Jesus Christ.

More Blessed to Give (Acts 20:25–35)

Paul knew that this was the last time he would ever see the Ephesian elders. As he said goodbye, he declared himself "innocent of the blood of all men" (Acts 20:26). Paul had declared to them the "whole purpose of God" (20:27). Sometimes we may be tempted to sugarcoat the gospel in an effort not to offend. Those efforts may cause us to fall short of presenting the whole truth of the gospel, that Jesus is the only way to the Father and that there is "no other name under heaven . . . by which we must be saved" (4:12). Paul had no such compunctions. As he said his farewells, he had the comfort of knowing that he had preached the entire gospel. If any did not receive Christ, their guilt was on their own heads. Those who chose not to follow Christ did not do so because they had not heard the truth.

Paul also urged these church leaders to be on their guard. The "overseers" or "elders" of the church had teaching and preaching responsibilities as well as shepherding or *pastoring* the church. Paul sometimes referred to these leaders as *stewards* of the flock (Titus 1:5–7). Paul had already battled with false teachers during his ministry, and he knew that after his departure even more "savage wolves" would attempt to lead the church astray. Some of these false teachers would even arise from within the congregation (Acts 20:30). Paul wanted the elders to be prepared to guard the church from this false teaching.

Paul wanted the Ephesian elders to follow his example in teaching sound doctrine, but he also wanted them to imitate the way in which he had lived among them. In New Testament times, many traveling teachers and healers sought to profit from their ministries. Paul was not one of these. During his three years in Ephesus, Paul did not seek to profit from the church. Rather, he worked with his own hands to support not only himself but also the other members of his ministry team (20:33–34). Paul had received his rabbinical training from Gamaliel, one of the most respected rabbis of his day. Paul also was a tentmaker by trade (18:1–3). During his time in Corinth, he worked as a tentmaker alongside Priscilla and Aquila.

It is likely that he supported himself in Ephesus in the same way.

Elsewhere Paul wrote that it is appropriate for Christian workers to be paid for their labors (1 Corinthians 9:9–14). Yet at times Paul did not claim this right, preferring to support himself. It seems that he had multiple reasons for doing so. One reason was that Paul did not want his actions to hinder the gospel, perhaps feeling that if he accepted payment for his labors some might dismiss him as being motivated by his own greed. Paul also desired to "offer the gospel without charge" (1 Cor. 9:18). He sought to offer an example to believers of how they should work to provide for their own needs rather than depending on handouts from the community (2 Thessalonians 3:7–10).

In reminding the elders of how he worked among them, Paul challenged their cultural norms. Paul labored not only to take care of himself but also to care for the entire community. Paul called them to follow him as he had followed Jesus, who said "it is more blessed to give than to receive" (Acts 20:35). Interestingly, this quote is not found in any of the Gospels. That does not mean it is not an authentic quote. We know that Jesus did more than the Gospels record (John 21:25). It is likely that Paul was quoting from an oral tradition of Jesus' teachings not preserved in written form. Regardless, the idea of giving without receiving anything in return was a foreign concept in the ancient world. Paul was challenging these elders to follow his example of giving without expectations. They were called to serve the weak, rather than forcing them to be servants. As they had received the gospel freely, they were now called to give without any thought of return.

Implications and Actions

Do you ever wonder what legacy you will leave behind? I am thankful for those in my family who preceded me in faith. As I walk in their footsteps, I am often mindful that my children will one day follow me in the same way.

Similarly, Paul called the Ephesian elders to follow in his footsteps and serve the church as he had served them. He served them with humility, seeking to bless rather than profit. Even in the face of opposition, he did not hesitate to boldly proclaim the full truth of the gospel. Now, Paul was saying goodbye, knowing full well that his obedience to God might cost him his life.

Selfishness comes naturally to most of us. When it comes to decisions like whether to serve, to witness, to give from our own time and resources, or to take a stand for the truth, we often wonder how it's going to affect us. If we don't like the answer, we don't follow through.

This passage challenges us to live differently—to give of ourselves because it is right, without considering what we might get in return. May we always remember that "it is more blessed to give than to receive" (Acts 20:35).

WILLIAM COLGATE: A GENEROUS LAYMAN

William Colgate (1783–1857), founder of Colgate-Palmolive, had a reputation for honesty, hard work, and fair business practices. He was also known for his generosity.

In the nineteenth century, many churches derived a large portion of their income from the practice of pew rental. The church where Colgate was a deacon rented pews. Colgate felt this limited access to the gospel and urged his church to abolish the practice. When giving did not replace the lost income, Colgate cheerfully balanced the books out of his own funds.

Colgate generously welcomed church visitors, often giving up his own seat to a visitor. During the revival of 1839–40, Colgate delegated his business to others so he could invest his time in visiting and discipling the large number of new believers. Throughout his life he gave to a variety of causes, including fully supporting a career missionary. Colgate's biographer calls his benevolence a matter of "religious conviction" and "an homage to God."[1]

CASE STUDY

Your church is in an area with high unemployment. Most of those looking for jobs have a low level of education or some quality such as a prison record or learning disability that makes finding work difficult. The few jobs that are available require skills that most people in your community do not have. How could your church be a blessing to the community in this situation?

QUESTIONS

1. What sometimes holds us back from declaring "the whole purpose of God"?

2. What are some of the ways Paul served as an example of generosity to the Ephesian church? How can we follow his example?

3. Paul challenged the Ephesian elders to give without expecting anything in return. When we give, are we sometimes guilty of asking, *What's in it for me?* What does it look like today to give without expectation of return?

4. Paul's service to the Ephesians was motivated by his love for God and his love for them. What message do we send in the way we serve?

NOTES

1. W. W. Everts, *William Colgate: A Christian Layman* (Philadelphia: American Baptist Publication Society, 1881), 248.

UNIT THREE

Examples That Warn

Unit three, "Examples That Warn," focuses on some of the warnings in Jesus' teachings about failing to live generously. The consequences of refusing to live generously are as tragic as the consequences of choosing to live generously are exhilarating.

UNIT THREE. EXAMPLES THAT WARN

FOCAL TEXT

Luke 12:13–21; 16:19–31;
James 5:1–6

BACKGROUND

Luke 12:13–21; 16:14–31;
James 5:1–6

LESSON EIGHT

Greedy and Insensitive Living

MAIN IDEA

Being unresponsive to others'
needs while selfishly accumulating
earthly treasures for ourselves
results ultimately in disaster.

QUESTION TO EXPLORE

What do you mean I can't use
what I have any way I want
to when I got it honestly?

STUDY AIM

To decide on ways I will respond to
the message that being unresponsive
to others' needs while selfishly
accumulating earthly treasures for
myself results ultimately in disaster

QUICK READ

All our wealth, no matter how much
or how little we may think we have,
will someday be left behind, and we
will answer for how we used it.

Barns used to be a big deal in the South where I grew up. Tobacco barns dotted the countryside, more numerous than houses. No farmer ever imagined forty years ago that the way of life on a tobacco farm would be reduced to nothing, and so they built more and more barns to increase their production and build their wealth.

Most of these barns sit unused these days, bearing silent but powerful testimony to a form of wealth that has dried up. The emptiness of those barns is haunting. Walk into one even now and you'll still smell the *bright leaf* curing there, but if you listen closely, you can also hear the wind whispering through the dilapidated walls the words of a rich man who once said, "I will pull down my barns and build larger ones" (Luke 12:18).[1]

LUKE 12:13–21

13 Someone in the crowd said to him, "Teacher, tell my brother to divide the family inheritance with me." **14** But he said to him, "Friend, who set me to be a judge or arbitrator over you?" **15** And he said to them, "Take care! Be on your guard against all kinds of greed; for one's life does not consist in the abundance of possessions." **16** Then he told them a parable: "The land of a rich man produced abundantly. **17** And he thought to himself, 'What should I do, for I have no place to store my crops?'

18 Then he said, 'I will do this: I will pull down my barns and build larger ones, and there I will store all my grain and my goods. **19** And I will say to my soul, Soul, you have ample goods laid up for many years; relax, eat, drink, be merry.' **20** But God said to him, 'You fool! This very night your life is being demanded of you. And the things you have prepared, whose will they be?' **21** So it is with those who store up treasures for themselves but are not rich toward God."

LUKE 16:19–31

19 "There was a rich man who was dressed in purple and fine linen and who feasted sumptuously every day. **20** And at his gate lay a poor man named Lazarus, covered with sores, **21** who longed to satisfy his hunger with what fell from the rich man's table; even the dogs would come and lick his sores. **22** The poor man died and was carried away by the angels to be with Abraham. The rich man also died and was buried. **23** In Hades, where he was being tormented, he looked up and saw Abraham far away with Lazarus by his side. **24** He called out, 'Father Abraham, have mercy on me, and send Lazarus to dip the tip of his finger in water and cool my tongue; for I am in agony in these flames.' **25** But Abraham said, 'Child, remember that during your lifetime you received your good things, and

Lazarus in like manner evil things; but now he is comforted here, and you are in agony. 26 Besides all this, between you and us a great chasm has been fixed, so that those who might want to pass from here to you cannot do so, and no one can cross from there to us.' 27 He said, 'Then, father, I beg you to send him to my father's house— 28 for I have five brothers—that he may warn them, so that they will not also come into this place of torment.' 29 Abraham replied, 'They have Moses and the prophets; they should listen to them.' 30 He said, 'No, father Abraham; but if someone goes to them from the dead, they will repent.' 31 He said to him, 'If they do not listen to Moses and the prophets, neither will they be convinced even if someone rises from the dead.'"

JAMES 5:1–6

1 Come now, you rich people, weep and wail for the miseries that are coming to you. 2 Your riches have rotted, and your clothes are moth-eaten. 3 Your gold and silver have rusted, and their rust will be evidence against you, and it will eat your flesh like fire. You have laid up treasure for the last days. 4 Listen! The wages of the laborers who mowed your fields, which you kept back by fraud, cry out, and the cries of the harvesters have reached the ears of the Lord of hosts. 5 You have lived on the earth in luxury and in pleasure; you have fattened your hearts in a day

of slaughter. **6** You have condemned and murdered the righteous one, who does not resist you.

Seeking Arbitration (Luke 12:13–15)

Our passage begins with a question for Jesus from a man in the crowd asking him to arbitrate the division of an estate. We assume it's a younger brother who is protesting that his older brother was getting a larger share of the estate, as Jewish law mandated. This younger brother obviously believed the ancient patriarchal law was unfair and hoped Jesus might set things on a more even playing field. But Jesus refused to enter into that fray. It wasn't because he feared conflict or because he was avoiding the role of arbitrator that was frequently associated with a rabbi in his culture.

Indeed, this younger brother was paying a compliment of sorts to Jesus. The man perceived that Jesus' teachings promoted fairness, and he perhaps hoped that Jesus would reinterpret this law as he had many others with a statement like, *You've heard it said, but I say. . . .* But that wasn't to happen that day. Jesus perceived the heart of the matter was really about greed. So he countered the younger brother's request with a warning: "Take care! Be on your guard against all kinds of greed; for one's life does not consist in the abundance of possessions" (Luke 12:15).

A Story to Reinforce the Warning (Luke 12:16–21)

The story of the rich barn-builder is easily visualized. See the grain pouring out of the tops of the old barn, overflowing to the ground. What was he to do with this abundance? The natural instinct was to find a way to preserve the grain, for it meant wealth and security for this man and his family. Who could blame him for preparing for an uncertain future? He could afford to build a bigger barn, and he'd worked hard. Having prepared for that uncertain future, wouldn't it be wonderful to kick back, relax, and enjoy the rest of his life in comfort?

His mistake, obvious to us, was not so obvious to him. He was rich in material goods, but he was not rich toward God. He did not acknowledge that the questions about barn size and economic security paled in comparison to the big questions of eternal security. This man was spiritually poor, and his overflowing barns were useless to him in death. You can almost hear the man's folly whispering through the barns, "relax, eat, drink, be merry" (12:19). It wouldn't have been long after his death that his great big barns were empty again.

The passage leaves the modern reader to ponder our emphasis on materialism, and the social status afforded to those who possess many things. As we wag our heads at the dead man with big barns, we should be suspect of our own accumulating in a world where many are in need.

Living generously for Jesus' sake is an idea that forces us to answer the question of how much is enough and to decide to direct our resources towards the poorest people.

Caring for the Poor (Luke 16:19–31)

In an exchange with some Pharisees known for their love of money (16:14), Jesus directed his ire at their conflicted value system with the strong words, "for what is prized by human beings is an abomination in the sight of God" (16:15). Mincing no words, Jesus was basically saying, *You've got it all backwards. Your economics are upside down, and here's an example of what I mean.*

Next came the *post mortem* on two men who died: a rich man with no name and a poor man named Lazarus. Up until his death, this rich man had been really living the high life. His purple clothes and fine linen were the signs of the wealthy of the day, and his sumptuous feasts were not for the occasional festival or party. He lived like this every day of the week. Just outside his gate lay Lazarus, so hungry that he craved the scraps from the rich man's table.

The incongruence of these two lives catches our attention. The Pharisees in Jesus' audience would have noticed also because they likely operated under a way of thinking that wealth signified God's blessing and poverty identified a lack of God's favor. For them, hearing that a rich man who by their theology was blessed by God but was now condemned to Hades made no sense. In their view, it should have been Lazarus who suffered and begged for a taste of water in the afterlife.

What caused the two men to die is not stated. It's also not certain whether the rich man would have been preserved from Hades had he tended to the needs of Lazarus. His indifference toward those who were hurting around him was ultimately a display of his inability to love the neighbor, which Jesus understood as part of the great commandment that included loving God. In this tale no amount of charity work done without love would ever suffice.

One might be tempted to read this passage to mean that the rich go to hell and the poor go to heaven. But that reading falls short of the story's rich capacity to help us see how important care for the poor is to God. Showing generosity to the poor and marginalized indicates not just our understanding of this theological truth, but also verifies the reality and the quality of our relationship to God.

The story challenges and chastises us to consider whether we, like the Pharisees, are *lovers of money* whose value system is so backwards that our wealth has become an abomination to God. Christians who pursue generosity for Jesus' sake will aim to divest themselves of luxuries and live more simply so that others in need may live well.

Warning Against Abuse of Wealth (James 5:1–6)

So far, we've examined two stories where Jesus seemed to frown on those who neglected basic spiritual principles of proper use of wealth. This passage from James addresses similar assumptions as those of the barn-builder in our first passage. The rich who were weeping over their lost treasures assumed that the world was predictable and controllable. They would find their treasures rotted, moth-eaten, and rusted. What's worse, these people had abused others in their acquisition of wealth. They had acted dishonestly, committing fraud and injustice toward the laborers. They had even murdered in order to build up their personal wealth. James warned that weeping and wailing were on the way for these rich abusers.

Committing such sins is exactly the opposite of generosity for Jesus' sake. When these sins are blatant, it is easy to judge, but what about times they aren't obvious or clear? For example, should American Christians purchase goods that are produced by laborers who are treated unfairly? Is it even possible in the global economic system to determine what is fairly made, or even what a fair wage is?

Christians must be held accountable for consuming goods that are produced at a profit on the backs of people who are abused and underpaid for their work. Christians should learn about how and what we consume. Churches should work together to see that fair trade is promoted and that people around the world are free of exploitation of their labor.[2] Failing to do so is silent complicity to the evil forces of greed at work in this world.

Implications and Actions

Admitting that we are *lovers of money* like the Pharisees is difficult. Maybe it's our neighbor's bigger house, pricey car, or sophisticated electronics that make us think we need more stuff. Even though we feel that we lack certain things, the reality is that we are very wealthy. The Bible passages explored today will not let us escape the reality that we live with an abundance beyond our needs and that we must pursue a simpler way of life. Even though we may have acquired our wealth through honest means, we are not free to spend and consume as we choose. Christians are called to a higher ethic of stewardship over the resources we have earned because we know that we have only been able to earn them by way of God's help.

Being generous beyond the basics of a tithe demonstrates our understanding that God is provider of all our resources, and that we have an obligation to treat our resources with care and thoughtfulness. But our generosity signals something more: it signals the reality of our trust in God that there will always be *enough* in the kingdom of God. When others see shortage and lack, our generosity turns the world's view on end and demonstrates that selflessness is not only the way of God, but it also is a way of life that is better for the world.

IDEAS FOR LIVING SIMPLY

Living simply is a great way to free yourself of greed and insensitive living. Living simply isn't complicated, but it can be hard. Here are six steps you can work on today to live more simply:

- Identify where you spend your time. Then list the top four or five priorities in your life. Ask God to help you order those priorities and step away from the things in life that are taking your attention from the top priorities.

- Identify who is important to you. Remember the stories from today's Bible lesson and ask God to reveal to you with whom you should spend your time and energy.

- Identify what material things are necessary in your life. Purge your house of all unnecessary things. If you haven't used a gadget in a year, consider giving it away. You may never miss the thing.

- Identify what habits you want to build into your life and what habits you want gone. Ask God to help you see the truth about things you think you just can't live without.

- Identify how you'll use your financial resources. Ask God to guide you in being generous for Jesus' sake.

- Ask God to guide you in your purchases. Create a decision-making system about purchases that allows for a *cooling off* period. If a thing costs more than $100 and isn't a regularly budgeted item, then wait a day. If it costs more than $1,000, wait a week. A good idea will also be a good idea later.

HADES

"Hades" is a term used in Luke 16 by Jesus to describe a place of torment. At that time the word "Hades" was equivalent to the Hebrew word *sheol*. In the Old Testament writings, *sheol* was the pit of darkness where all the dead go regardless of their moral choices. Jesus' use of "Hades" as a place of fire and pain was a new understanding of the afterlife, and different from that of his fellow Jews. It certainly would have caught their attention and put clear emphasis on aid for the poor having a significant consequence in the afterlife.

QUESTIONS

1. What *bigger barns* are in your life? What things have you purchased thinking they would make your life easier and more comfortable and yet have found that they only clutter your world now? What would it take for you to release those things to God? to others in need?

2. Does more money equal more or less stress about money in your experience?

3. Is it too far-fetched to examine every good or service you buy to ensure that you are not abusing others with your everyday consumption?

4. How much more would you pay for a computer to ensure it is built ethically and that the workers are paid a living wage? How much more for a cup of coffee? a pound of tomatoes?

NOTES

1. Unless otherwise indicated, all Scripture quotations in "Introducing Living Generously for Jesus' Sake," lesson 8–13, and the introductions to units 3 and 4 are taken from the New Revised Standard Version Bible.

2. For more information, see http://goodnewsgoods.com/educational-resources/fair-trade-facts/ Accessed 3/1/12.

FOCAL TEXT
Mark 10:17–31

BACKGROUND
Mark 10:17–31

LESSON NINE

Choosing Stuff over Jesus

MAIN IDEA

Putting possessions ahead of following
Jesus leads to a tragic result.

QUESTION TO EXPLORE

Your money or your life—
which will it be?

STUDY AIM

To evaluate what my actions show
to be the relative importance of
Jesus and possessions in my life

QUICK READ

Being generous for Jesus' sake
means leaving the material stuff
behind in exchange for a life
that is full of spiritual riches.

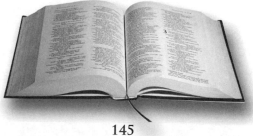

The words, "how hard it will be for those who have wealth to enter the kingdom of God!" (Mark 10:23), brought me a sigh of relief when I was a young Christian. Jesus said it was difficult for a rich person to enter the kingdom of God, and so, being dirt poor, I had a definite advantage. Looking back, I realize I had missed the point: I was still materialistic, obsessed with things. My obsession was with things I didn't have.

Now I have more things in my life than I want. When I moved across the country a few years ago, my moving truck weighed in at just under 15,000 pounds. My household goods were going into storage for a few months, and I said more than once, "Wouldn't it be wonderful if the movers lost all our stuff? We'd be free of our junk and rid of our materialism." But I was only talking a big game; I know what would have happened. Eventually I would have replaced all those possessions with more stuff.

We are soothed by our possessions because we falsely trust them for comfort. And now, when I read this passage, I am no less disturbed by my possession obsession.

MARK 10:17–31

17 As he was setting out on a journey, a man ran up and knelt before him, and asked him, "Good Teacher, what must I do to inherit eternal life?" **18** Jesus said to him, "Why do you call me good? No one is good but God alone. [19] You know the commandments: 'You shall not murder; You shall not commit adultery; You shall not steal; You shall not bear false witness; You shall not defraud; Honor your father and mother.'" [20] He said to him, "Teacher, I have kept all these since my youth." [21] Jesus, looking at him, loved him and said, "You lack one thing; go, sell what you own, and give the money to the poor, and you will have treasure in heaven; then come, follow me." [22] When he heard this, he was shocked and went away grieving, for he had many possessions.

[23] Then Jesus looked around and said to his disciples, "How hard it will be for those who have wealth to enter the kingdom of God!" [24] And the disciples were perplexed at these words. But Jesus said to them again, "Children, how hard it is to enter the kingdom of God! [25] It is easier for a camel to go through the eye of a needle than for someone who is rich to enter the kingdom of God." [26] They were greatly astounded and said to one another, "Then who can be saved?" [27] Jesus looked at them and said, "For mortals it is impossible, but not for God; for God all things are possible."

[28] Peter began to say to him, "Look, we have left everything and followed you." [29] Jesus said, "Truly I tell you, there is no one who has left house or brothers or sisters or mother or father or children or fields, for my sake and for the sake of the good news, [30] who will not receive a hundredfold now in this age—houses, brothers and sisters, mothers and children, and fields, with

persecutions—and in the age to come eternal life. [31] But
many who are first will be last, and the last will be first."

The Possession Obsession (Mark 10:17–22)

A rich man approached Jesus seeking answers for difficult problems. The other Gospels variously call him rich,
young, and a ruler (see Matthew 19:16–30; Luke 18:18–30).
Mark described him simply as a man with many possessions who kept the commandments.

The man ran up to Jesus, knelt before him in rever-
ence, and asked how to inherit eternal life. He called
Jesus "Good Teacher," but Jesus rejected the title "good,"
signaling that the word "good" was for God alone. Jesus
continued his response without pause, pointing out what
the rich man already knew. *Keep the commandments*,
Jesus said. The man's response was that he had done all
those things since he was young.

The man's answer hinted at something a modern
reader has likely already discovered. Having kept the law,
he still doubted his spiritual vitality. He wondered about
eternal life even though he had kept the commands faith-
fully. The implied question, *What else must I do?*, haunts
many believers in Jesus. The implied question betrays the
doubt that God's gift of grace is really sufficient for salvation, and the question expresses a desire to *do* something
in order to inherit eternal life.

In this moment, the normally sparse and *in-a-hurry* Gospel of Mark pauses. If this scene were being acted out in a movie, Jesus would stop walking, look at the rich man, and fully consider him. When Jesus beheld this man, we are told that Jesus "loved him." Seeing the man's inability to realize he could do nothing to earn God's favor, Jesus' emotions were obvious to everyone around. It's almost as if Jesus, eyes smiling and compassionate, saw with the eyes of God how humans have struggled since creation to earn their way back into paradise. This was a moment of intimacy between God and humanity. As Jesus looked closely at the man, Jesus perceived the problem: the man was hung up on his earthly treasures.

This exchange exposes the human weakness for things and the human inability to save self. Jesus' disciples were about to learn the only way by which a person can inherit eternal life: by way of God's miracle. The man walked away, grieved and shocked. What was demanded of him was incomprehensible, and so he went away sad.

God's Possibilities or Our Possessions (Mark 10:23–27)

The central issue of eternal life as it related to the man's possessions leaves us with a hard question. If he were unwilling to give up his possessions, did it become impossible for him to inherit eternal life? And is this the plan for us as well? This seems to be the question that Jesus was addressing in the next section of Scripture.

Turning to his disciples, Jesus stated that it is difficult for those with wealth to enter the kingdom of God. But is it simply because of the wealth? Is it truly impossible for a rich person to enter the kingdom? Jesus pressed further with an illustration that it was easier for a camel to go through the eye of a needle than for a rich man to enter the kingdom. Some interpreters have suggested that this illustration refers to a special gate in the city wall of Jerusalem, but this seems doubtful. Evidence for such a gate in the time of Jesus is lacking. It is likely that Jesus was speaking figuratively, as he did in Matthew 23:24 in reference to the Pharisees straining out a gnat but swallowing a camel. Like the plank in the eye, what we have here is an example of Hebrew hyperbole.

These various explanations are attempts to minimize what Jesus was trying to say about the difficulty of being both wealthy and a disciple of Jesus. We must understand this tough saying of Jesus as his teaching about wealth as a barrier to discipleship and kingdom living, as are other things like power, prestige, and influence. Even if we could be as devout as the rich man who kept all the other commandments, there will always be at least *something* that disqualifies us from a completely holy life, *something* that prevents us from earning our way into God's grace. And that seems to be the point.

Humans need God's miracle of grace in order to live in God's kingdom. Humans need the miracle of Jesus' death on the cross as a final and ultimate offering for sin. Whether it's wealth or something else, there are always barriers to our discipleship, barriers to our loyalty to Jesus and his peculiar kingdom. So it is best for us to trust that the kingdom is something God will do, not we for ourselves.

Give It Up Now, Live It Up Later (Mark 10:28–31)

Sometimes words on a page do not do justice to the emotion they are meant to convey. Peter had had it up to his eyeballs with all this confusing talk about riches and camels through eyes of needles. It had stopped making sense to him. "Look," he said, "we have left everything and followed you" (Mark 10:28).

Peter seemed to think that since he had already given up his material wealth to follow Jesus that he was in the kingdom of God by default. In this regard, he had made the same mistake as the possession-laden man who went away sad, for they had both trusted in their own means as a way of entering into the kingdom of God.

Jesus offered an alternative view. *Oh yes, Peter, you are going to receive back all that you left behind for my sake; by a hundred-fold, in fact. But these blessings will be because of a new life in the kingdom of God. The people of God's kingdom will become the new family of those who follow Jesus completely. The kingdom of God will become your house and your field.*

And Jesus added something else—persecutions. This wrinkle adds a dimension to the cost of discipleship. Not only will there be things we must give up in order to follow Jesus fully, but there may also be additional costs we cannot anticipate. There may be suffering in addition to the giving up of stuff. Although investing our lives in following Jesus will bring us rewards, Jesus did not promise that those rewards would be material.

Implications and Actions

Resisting the pressures of the consumer culture around us is difficult for Christians. Advertising blares, *You earned it; you deserve it!* We have even been told the best way to help our economy is to spend more money. But Christians are to strive for a simpler lifestyle that is not dominated by the purchase of things or maintaining them. Instead, we are to seek a lifestyle that leaves us free to follow and serve Jesus.

Possessions are dangerous to the Christian life because they have two kinds of associated costs: the price tag—what you pay monetarily—and the hidden costs. The hidden costs are time, stress, and maintenance. Buy a bigger house and it takes longer to clean. Buy a luxury car and you worry about where to park so it won't get stolen or damaged. All the toys of life are significantly more expensive than the upfront costs. With few exceptions, those expenses take a toll on our spiritual life, our service to the kingdom of God, and our relationship with Jesus.

CASE STUDY

A family with teenagers buys a recreational boat to spend more time together. The family gets out on Saturdays in the summer and grows closer. However, the wife, a leader in their church, has missed several community service days at the church. In addition, the Saturday trips are more frequently becoming Saturday and Sunday trips, taking the family out of church on Sundays. Instead of attending worship, the family prays together, has a Bible reading, and then hits the lake.

You are good friends with one of the spouses, and you've even enjoyed a relaxing boat ride with them on occasion. They express a twinge of concern to you about missing church. How do you respond? Has the boat become a possession that distracts the family from the kingdom of God? Is there an acceptable balance of recreation and service? How do you find it?

MINIMALISM

Minimalism is a concept of living with no possessions except necessary ones. Supporters of the idea say that they feel freer, more creative, and less stressed. Can you imagine a life free of worry about possessions? No worries about maintenance, theft, or insurance. There is power in *less*. Brainstorm a list of the things you absolutely need to live a happy life.

QUESTIONS

1. What are some challenges in your spiritual life that separate you from God?

2. In Mark 10:21, Jesus looked at the man and "loved him." What is special about this phrase? What would it feel like for you to experience fully Jesus' love in that kind of encounter?

3. Wealth is one barrier to discipleship. What are other barriers you can name?

4. Inherent in this story is the idea that being generous for Jesus' sake with our possessions eliminates one barrier to our entering the kingdom of God. In what ways does this make us free? What possessions in your life are distracting you from God? What should you do?

5. Jesus lists persecution as a benefit for those who give up their lives for the sake of the good news. How can persecution be a benefit?

FOCAL TEXT
Matthew 25:31–46

BACKGROUND
Matthew 25:31–46

LESSON TEN
Failing to Be Generous

MAIN IDEA

Failing to extend generous care
to even the lowliest and neediest
of people indicates that we
really do not care for Jesus.

QUESTION TO EXPLORE

Why should we stoop to serve the
lowliest and neediest of people?

STUDY AIM

To identify ways God is calling
me to extend generous care to all
people, even people I may consider
the lowliest and neediest

QUICK READ

Being generous for Jesus' sake
will matter in the judgment to
come, and deeds of love and
mercy are what count.

You don't have to hang around a barnyard or be a shepherd to tell the difference between sheep and goats. The differences are obvious, even to a city slicker. Matthew 25 teaches that Jesus will return one day and separate people like a shepherd separates sheep and goats. But the differences that Jesus will see in people aren't as obvious as the differences we see. Jesus will apply different criteria, ones that matter a great deal. Let us consider these criteria and what they mean to be generous for Jesus' sake.

MATTHEW 25:31–46

31 "When the Son of Man comes in his glory, and all the angels with him, then he will sit on the throne of his glory. 32 All the nations will be gathered before him, and he will separate people one from another as a shepherd separates the sheep from the goats, 33 and he will put the sheep at his right hand and the goats at the left. 34 Then the king will say to those at his right hand, 'Come, you that are blessed by my Father, inherit the kingdom prepared for you from the foundation of the world; 35 for I was hungry and you gave me food, I was thirsty and you gave me something to drink, I was a stranger and you welcomed me, 36 I was naked and you gave me clothing, I was sick and you took care of me, I was in prison and you visited me.' 37 Then the righteous will answer him, 'Lord, when was it that we saw you hungry and gave you food, or thirsty and gave

you something to drink? **38** And when was it that we saw you a stranger and welcomed you, or naked and gave you clothing? **39** And when was it that we saw you sick or in prison and visited you?' **40** And the king will answer them, 'Truly I tell you, just as you did it to one of the least of these who are members of my family, you did it to me.' **41** Then he will say to those at his left hand, 'You that are accursed, depart from me into the eternal fire prepared for the devil and his angels; **42** for I was hungry and you gave me no food, I was thirsty and you gave me nothing to drink, **43** I was a stranger and you did not welcome me, naked and you did not give me clothing, sick and in prison and you did not visit me.' **44** Then they also will answer, 'Lord, when was it that we saw you hungry or thirsty or a stranger or naked or sick or in prison, and did not take care of you?' **45** Then he will answer them, 'Truly I tell you, just as you did not do it to one of the least of these, you did not do it to me.' **46** And these will go away into eternal punishment, but the righteous into eternal life."

As We Gather Around the Throne (Matt. 25:31–34)

The passage opens dramatically: the Son of Man arrives in all his glory, angels in the entourage, and sits on a throne. The passage warns Matthew's readers about what to expect when Jesus returns. He will be seated on his throne, surrounded by angels.

He will be discriminating, although not in the usual way. The hearers of Jesus' story normally would have been put at ease with the line found in verse 32, "All the nations will be gathered before him, and he will separate people one from another." *Aha!* these Jews would be thinking. Rubbing their hands together in anticipation of the smack-down that Jesus was about to give the Gentiles, the Jews would have been expecting a wonderful separation story of sheep and goats based on ethnic lines. Instead, he would separate people based on their actions. Specifically, he is going to assign status in the barnyard of the kingdom of God based on acts of service to the least and lowest of society. Both the sheep and the goats are surprised by their categorical assignment.

Sheep and Their Good Deeds (Matt. 25:35–40)

That Jesus preferred the sheep is obvious. Entrance to this group requires only one thing: simple acts of kindness toward the least and lowest. But let us be careful lest we slip into a works-based faith. It doesn't seem likely that Jesus wanted disciples to keep score of their good deeds. If that were the case he likely would have picked bigger acts of kindness to illustrate his purposes, not simple things like a drink of water, a welcome handshake, or a set of clothes.

Jesus wanted his followers to keep working at these acts of kindness because he understood that the disciples would be his emissaries after he left earth. The dividing of people into sheep and goats is less about judgment and more about encouragement. The story is meant to motivate Jesus' hearers to see that living in the kingdom is less about laws and rituals and more about right relationships to all people—even the lowest and the least. Later, the Apostle Paul would extend this thinking to the church at Corinth when he wrote:

> All this is from God, who reconciled us to himself through Christ, and has given us the ministry of reconciliation; that is, in Christ God was reconciling the world to himself, not counting their trespasses against them, and entrusting the message of reconciliation to us. So we are ambassadors for Christ, since God is making his appeal through us; we entreat you on behalf of Christ, be reconciled to God (2 Corinthians 5:18–20).

God invites believers to take part in the redeeming work of Christ. Paul referred to Christians as ambassadors who bear a message of reconciliation. Jesus taught that one way disciples do this is by serving the least and lowest, with no regard for status. We become sheep who reconcile the world to God with our tiny acts of kindness.

Recognizing this class of reconciling sheep makes clear that what we do as Christians matters. Yes, our salvation is based on faith and not works, but what we do after our salvation in service builds our relationship with Jesus and our understanding of the world in which we live. When we are other-directed and outwardly-focused in our faith, we see the world differently, with more compassion and care. By faith we are saved, and in faith we serve. Further, our service opens the way for others to come into saving knowledge of Jesus. Then, as our service to the world stretches, we come to view the world more like God looks at us—with compassion and mercy. The transcendent Christ appears in the sheep and is therefore alive in the world.

Goats and Their Sins of Omission (Matt. 25:41–46)

No one in Jesus' day would have wanted to be compared to a goat. Even without Jesus' explanation that the goats did nothing to care for the least and lowliest, everyone knew that goats were less desirable than sheep.

At the throne, the king would tell these goats why they were goats: they had failed to pass along the simple acts of kindness to people in need. Jesus described how they, in mirror opposition to the sheep, failed to give him food, clothing, water, or compassion whenever they failed to do it for "the least of these." The question they asked would be the reverse of the question the sheep asked: "When was it that we saw you hungry or thirsty or a stranger or naked or sick or in prison, and did not take care of you?"

(Matthew 25:44; compare 25:38–39). Whereas the sheep were filled with joy and ushered into the blessing of the Father as inheritors of the kingdom, the goats would be cast out into the eternal fire prepared for the devil and his angels.

The image of sheep caring for a broken world stands in stark opposition to goats who pass through life unfazed and unaware of the world's pain. While the goats didn't do anything explicitly hurtful, their sin of not noticing landed them in the eternal flame. These are sins of omission.

Jesus had a connection with the suffering of the world because he identified and entered into it. If our relationship with Jesus is genuine, we must extend generous care to those who suffer. These goats missed Jesus because they failed to notice the suffering.

Implications and Actions

Jesus told this story of separation with high hopes that we would take the initiative and be motivated to become sheep by our actions. Because we have this story, we do not need to be surprised at the Day of Judgment. We carry within us an understanding of what we should do because of this story. Disciples of Jesus who desire to be generous must do so without regard for the status of the persons in need. Because people of this world encounter the living Christ through his disciples, our intentionality to care for the least of those in the world matters.

While we cannot meet every need in the world, God enables us to meet some needs. It may be tempting to despair and withhold generosity because we cannot solve every problem, but we sheep must be compelled to try. The efforts need not be extravagant or far-reaching. A drink of water, a hospital visit, or a jail visit are small but significant ways of serving Jesus himself. We don't have to flex our imagination much to come up with other small acts of kindness that have a huge impact on the kingdom of God.

It's important to understand that Jesus is always in our midst. Opportunities abound to serve Jesus and his children. Sometimes he is there in the face of the homeless beggar; other times he appears more subtly in the form of a friend in need of a listening ear, or even a child in need of our time and affirmation. *Living Generously for Jesus' Sake* is the title of our study series, and today's biblical text models with unmistakable clarity what it means to be generous for Jesus' sake.

PAROUSIA

Parousia, a word that simply means *presence* or *arrival,* is used throughout the New Testament to refer to the return of Jesus. This return will signify the arrival of God's kingdom on earth, a time at which people will meet with judgment from God.

Because Matthew's Gospel was written after Jesus' death and resurrection, Matthew blended the time Jesus was physically present with the future unknown time of Jesus' return. Today's story is a perfect example of this blending, as Matthew has Jesus telling about a time in the future when he would return to fulfill his kingdom. As such, it reminds us that giving even the littlest kindness to the least is an important thing to be doing while we await the *parousia*. To be generous for Jesus' sake necessarily means that we care for the lowliest and neediest of all God's children.

SON OF MAN

The Son of Man is a title used by Jesus of himself in the Gospels. Others assigned him this title, as well. The New Testament offers no clear explanation of the meaning of the name, but it has multiple associations.

- In some passages, it is appropriate to interpret the name's meaning as *future man*, as in the one who will rule in God's kingdom to come.

- In Old Testament literature, the name seems to have a messianic meaning, and so it serves as a type of foreshadowing for Jesus.

- Sometimes the passages that include the name are about the Son of Man's mission on earth, along with predictions of his crucifixion and his future return.

- In John, the title competes with the "I am" sayings as a way of better understanding Jesus' nature.

The phrase has been debated for a long time, and there is no clear consensus on its exact meaning. Some scholars think it was simply a messianic title in Jesus' day.[1]

QUESTIONS

1. The sheep in this story perform good deeds without a conscious effort to do so. It's as if they're on *autopilot*. What changes would you have to make to perform care in such a way?

2. Why do you sometimes fail to notice the needs of others around you?

3. Is it possible for a *goat* to become a *sheep?* If so, how? If not, why not?

4. What examples of ministry do you see in your church that meet the criteria Jesus sets forth toward caring for *the least of these?*

5. How would other aspects of your life change if you started to notice the needs of others more frequently?

NOTES ────────────────────────────────

1. Bruce Metzger & Michael Coogan, eds., "Son of Man," *The Oxford Companion to the Bible* (New York, NY: Oxford University Press, 1993), 711–713.

—— U N I T   F O U R ——
You Can Live Generously

Unit four, "You Can Live Generously," provides lessons on living generously in three areas of our lives. Because of our gracious, generous God, we can live generously in our relationships, with our gifts, and, yes, with our material possessions.

UNIT FOUR. YOU CAN LIVE GENEROUSLY

FOCAL TEXT

Colossians 3:12–14;
Hebrews 13:1–8, 14–16

BACKGROUND

Colossians 3:12–14;
Hebrews 13:1–16

LESSON ELEVEN

Be Generous in Your Relationships

MAIN IDEA

Christians are to demonstrate kindness and love generously in all the relationships of their lives.

QUESTION TO EXPLORE

How are you showing kindness and love in the relationships of your life?

STUDY AIM

To decide how I will demonstrate kindness and love generously in the relationships of my life

QUICK READ

Godly virtues and love are essential ingredients for wholesome relationships. They are expressed in remembering others and sharing generously with them because of Jesus' sacrifice.

Studying biblical Hebrew is challenging and repetitious for most seminary students. I never expected the lesson I (Renate) learned one fall day in 1996. One of my classmates, a beautiful and brilliant Korean woman, made an astonishing statement. Her words are forever etched in my memory.

Although she struggled with the English language, she excelled in Hebrew and outscored everyone in the class. Because English was not her first language, she did not always understand the professor's questions. On one occasion my exasperated professor asked why she insisted on studying Hebrew in America. I held my breath as she explained that after Hebrew, she also intended to master Greek so she could explain the Bible from the original text. She continued that later in Korea, sometime during the winter, at night, when the border guards would least expect it, she would climb into a tube and lower herself into a flowing river at the North and South Korean border. She would then float into North Korea. There she would share the gospel and teach the Bible to her brothers and sisters.

The class stared at her in disbelief. Finally, one of the other students asked, "Is that not dangerous? Won't they kill you if they capture you?" She smiled with sweet determination and answered, "I will go. I have much; they nothing." I had never seen such sacrificial generosity up close. I have never seen it since.

Among God's people, generosity is most explicitly observed in sacrificial attitudes toward others. The Bible teaches us to be generous in our relationships in various ways.

COLOSSIANS 3:12–14

[12] As God's chosen ones, holy and beloved, clothe yourselves with compassion, kindness, humility, meekness, and patience. [13] Bear with one another and, if anyone has a complaint against another, forgive each other; just as the Lord has forgiven you, so you also must forgive. [14] Above all, clothe yourselves with love, which binds everything together in perfect harmony.

HEBREWS 13:1–8, 14–16

[1] Let mutual love continue. [2] Do not neglect to show hospitality to strangers, for by doing that some have entertained angels without knowing it. [3] Remember those who are in prison, as though you were in prison with them; those who are being tortured, as though you yourselves were being tortured. [4] Let marriage be held in honor by all, and let the marriage bed be kept undefiled; for God will judge fornicators and adulterers. [5] Keep your lives

free from the love of money, and be content with what you have; for he has said, "I will never leave you or forsake you." **6** So we can say with confidence,

"The Lord is my helper;

I will not be afraid.

What can anyone do to me?"

7 Remember your leaders, those who spoke the word of God to you; consider the outcome of their way of life, and imitate their faith. **8** Jesus Christ is the same yesterday and today and forever.

• •

14 For here we have no lasting city, but we are looking for the city that is to come. **15** Through him, then, let us continually offer a sacrifice of praise to God, that is, the fruit of lips that confess his name. **16** Do not neglect to do good and to share what you have, for such sacrifices are pleasing to God.

God's People Clothe Themselves with Love (Col. 3:12–14)

In Colossians 3, Paul urged believers to focus on the things of Christ. Using Greek rhetoric, he commanded them to accept godly virtues, which he listed alongside worldly vices (Colossians 3:5–17).[1] The list of vices contains examples of the old life that must be stripped off in order that they would clothe themselves with the new self (Col. 3:5–10). The metaphor of taking off and putting on clothing was common, and the concept communicated well in the ancient world.[2]

Paul presented eight overall virtues, the superior of which is love (3:12–14). The first five virtues are grouped together (3:12). These virtues are contrasted with five vices (3:5).[3]

The first four of these vices in verse five are sexual in nature. The fifth vice, "greed, which is idolatry," likewise might have sexual overtones since "idolatry" was widespread and included sexual rituals.[4] "Passion" likely referred to an insatiable appetite for unrestrained sexual pleasures.[5]

The five Christ-like virtues in verse 12 are listed as the godly counterparts to the vices. These virtues (3:12) are each found in the Bible as characteristic of the life and ministry of Christ.

The five virtues listed in verse 12 are "compassion, kindness, humility, meekness, and patience." God's chosen ones are to put on the Christ-like virtue of "compassion." In the original language this word reads *bowels of compassion*. For the ancients, the seat of emotions was found in the bowels. Jesus demonstrated this sense of compassion when he saw a great crowd who were like sheep without a shepherd (Mark 6:34).

Next, God's chosen ones are to put on kindness. This virtue is also listed in Paul's list of vices and virtues in Galatians 5:19–23.

Furthermore, Christians must clothe themselves with "humility" and serve one another (Col. 3:12). Fourth, the word translated "meekness" is also translated "gentleness" (NASB). Christ himself stated that he was "gentle and humble in heart" (Matthew 11:29). Gentleness, Christ stated, characterized the core of his being. God's chosen ones ought to follow in Christ's footsteps by taking on these same virtues.

The last of the five virtues mentioned in verse twelve is "patience." This virtue is also part of the lists of vices and virtues in Galatians (Gal. 5:19–23). Paul connected another virtue with patience by stating, "Love is patient" (1 Cor. 13:4). True love is seen in the very character of God (2 Peter 3:9).

The believers in Colossae were to bear with one another and forgive one another when wronged (Col. 3:13). As long as the believers appeared to want to put on the virtues, others were to bear with their flaws. However, this approach was tempered by the teaching in Colossians 2. Believers must not bear false teachings.[6]

Above all, God's chosen ones clothe themselves with love (3:14). Whatever had been damaged and whoever had been wronged, only love offered healing. This charge harkens back to the greatest commandment, voiced by Christ himself: "You shall love the Lord your God with all your heart, and with all your soul, and with all your mind, and with all your strength. . . . You shall love your neighbor as yourself" (Mark 12:30–31). If God's people allow themselves to be clothed with Christ, love will bind the fellowship together in perfect harmony (Col. 3:14).

God's People Remember Others (Heb. 13:1–8)

Near the end of Hebrews 12, the believers were reminded that they had come to Jesus, the mediator of a new covenant (Hebrews 12:24). Moreover, Christians received "a kingdom that cannot be shaken" (Heb. 12:28). The opening verse of Hebrews 13 spurs on believers to "let mutual love continue" (13:1). "The kingdom that cannot be shaken" in chapter 12 is realized in mutual love among the believers.[7] The term used in the original language that is translated as "mutual love" is *philadelphia*. The term indicates a strong bond, the kind of love characteristic of that found between siblings.[8]

God's people were expected to remember a key social feature: hospitality to traveling strangers (13:2). Jesus spoke about this very practice in his parable about the sheep and the goats (Matt. 25:35, 38, 43–44; see lesson 10).[9] The exhortation in Hebrews 13:2 is reinforced by an allusion ("entertained angels without knowing it") to the story in Genesis about Abraham and Sarah. They welcomed three visitors, of whom at least two turned out to be heavenly messengers (Genesis 18:1–33; see also 19:1).

In the same parable of the sheep and the goats, Jesus spoke about visiting those in prison (Matt. 25:36, 39,

43–44). Thus, God's people are to "remember those who are in prison" (Heb. 13:2). In the parable, Jesus referred to the "least" among people, such as prisoners (Matt. 25:40). Indeed, imprisoned Christians were often looked upon with shame (2 Timothy 1:8). Yet Christians ought not to worry about status in this world. Rather, they are to identify with Christians who underwent unjust suffering (Heb. 13:3). Believers who live such a lifestyle set a Christ-like example for the world. Such an example also includes sexual purity, marital fidelity, and contentment "with what you have" (13:4–5). For the believers to whom Hebrews was written, this was a stark contrast with the surrounding pagan world in which sexual immorality and envy were rampant. The believers were able to stand in this environment because the Lord himself would help them (13:5–6).

Further, God's people are to remember their leaders, especially those who first "spoke the word of God" to them (13:7). Examples of lives exhibiting great faith were given in Hebrews 11. Believers were challenged to remember current or recent leaders. These leaders preached the word and thus perhaps were the founders of the church. The believers specifically were to observe the "outcome" of the lives of these leaders and to "imitate their faith" (13:7). "The outcome of their way of life" may refer to martyrdom.[10] Like the heroes in Hebrews 11, these leaders too held onto the promises of God (11:32–40). God's promise to be with them remains (Heb. 13:8; Matt. 28:20).

God's People Share Generously (Heb. 13:9–16)

God's people were to focus on grace rather than on religious ceremonial regulations (Heb. 13:9). They were to focus on the faith of the leaders and the grace exhibited, rather than on strange teachings.

Verses 10–11 use the tabernacle ritual as powerful imagery for presenting the ultimate sacrifice—Christ. Connecting the food regulations mentioned in verse 9 with this imagery, verse 10 refers to ritual sacrifices on the Day of Atonement.[11] On the Day of Atonement, the sacrifices were not eaten but rather burned outside the camp (13:11). The burning took place there because leftover sacrifices were considered unclean. Sin offerings were likewise burned outside the camp (Exodus 29:14). Nothing unclean could enter the holy place.

The author makes his argument in verse 12 by applying the analogy to Christ and stating, "Therefore Jesus also suffered outside the city." In light of previous verses, Jesus is presented here as a sin offering. Moreover, he was crucified outside of Jerusalem (Matt. 27:32a; Mark 15:20b; Luke 23:32–33; John 19:17). As the blood of a bull was applied to the altar for the forgiveness of the people's sins (Exod. 29:10–12), Christ sanctified the people with his blood. The believers were encouraged to follow Jesus in a similar way (Heb. 13:13). Going outside the camp is a euphemism for bearing shame, as outside the camp was an unclean place. Crucifixion was a shameful death, reserved for slaves and insurrectionists. Thus, following Jesus means following him in his shame. Hebrews recognizes this, stating, "Let us . . . bear the abuse he endured" (13:13). The believers were facing abuse but were encouraged to follow Christ regardless of potential suffering.

In verse 14, the believers are given an outlook beyond their situation—a sacrifice of praise, confessing Christ's name (13:15). Too, they are to do good and show generosity (13:16). Following Jesus outside the camp leads to generous, even sacrificial, sharing.

Implications and Actions

Christ-like virtues are inseparable from healthy relationships. These virtues express themselves in serving others and sharing generously as Christ has shared himself with us. Because of Christ's love, Christians must lay aside old ways of life and take up the new life. This life should be obvious to the world and should be characterized by a lifestyle of love that manifests Christ's life and teaching. Because of Christ's example of love, there remains no room in the Christian life for holding grudges. For Christians, love has become the norm of life, not an exception or a whim.

Christ's love, characterized by such qualities as kindness and humility, should mobilize us to develop unity in fellowship and generosity in relationships. The generosity that comes naturally to our transformed hearts should motivate us to go beyond the church walls. Christ-like generosity should cause Christians to serve in many situations, ranging from helping the lowly of the world to nurturing a wholesome family life. Generosity springs from a sacrificial heart, exemplified by our Lord Christ who gave himself on the cross for us.

HOSPITALITY IN BIBLE TIMES

In the world of the Bible, hospitality was never about welcoming family and friends into the home. Rather, it was about interacting with strangers.[12] One was to care for the needs of strangers as if they were friends. Inns were costly and often housed prostitutes and bandits.[13] Hospitality had become a key social value in Israel and the Greco-Roman world in the first century. Hospitality became a part of Christian values as well. The world watched to see whether Christians extended hospitality to strangers. Jesus referred to this act as a litmus test for his true followers (Matt. 25:35, 38, 40, 43–46).

In that day, traveling preachers needed places to stay. At times these were people who carried a social stigma and might bring this stigma to the home, in which case reputations were decreased. Perhaps this situation is in view in Hebrews 13:2. However, this custom could lead to housing false teachers. Discernment was needed to know

the difference between sound preachers and those to
whom hospitality should not be extended (2 John 7–11).

QUESTIONS

1. Colossians 3:14 states, "Above all, clothe yourselves
   with love. . . ." Why is love so important among
   Christians?

2. What role does forgiveness play in the church? How
   have you seen it at work in the church?

3. Would you say that the church truly resembles a family? Why? Why not? How can you contribute or make a difference?

4. Hospitality was a key custom in the biblical world. What are some customs in today's culture in America that, when embraced by Christians, provide an opportunity to share our faith?

5. In what way does Jesus' sacrifice spur you on to generous sharing?

NOTES

1. Ben Witherington, *The Letters to Philemon, The Colossians, and the Ephesians; A Socio-Rhetorical Commentary on the Captivity Epistles* (Grand Rapids: MI: William B. Eerdmans Publishing Company, 2007), 174–175.

2. Clinton E. Arnold, Frank S. Thielman, and S. M. Baugh, *Zondervan Illustrated Bible Backgrounds Commentary: Ephesians, Philippian, Colossians, Philemon* (Grand Rapids, MI: Zondervan, 2002), 96–97.

3. Witherington, 175–176.

4. Unless otherwise indicated, all Scripture quotations in "Introducing Living Generously for Jesus' Sake," lessons 8–13, and the introductions to units 3 and 4 are taken from the New Revised Standard Version Bible.

5. Arnold, 96.

6. Arnold, 97.

7. Edgar V. McKnight and Christopher Church, *Smyth and Helwys Bible Commentary: Hebrews-James* (Mason, GA: Smyth & Helwys Publishing, Inc., 2004), 307.

8. David A. Desilva, *Perseverance in Gratitude: A Socio-Rhetorical Commentary on the Epistle to the Hebrews* (Grand Rapids, MI: William B. Eerdmans Publishing Company, 2000), 485.

9. See also 1 Tim. 3:2; 1 Pet. 4:9.

10. DeSilva, 494.

11. McKnight, 311.

12. John J. Pilch and Bruce J. Malina, eds., *Handbook of Biblical Social Values* (Peabody, MA: Hendrickson Publishers, Inc., 1998), 115.

13. George H. Guthrie and Douglas J. Moo, *Zondervan Illustrated Bible Backgrounds Commentary: Hebrews, James* (Grand Rapids, MI: Zondervan, 2002), 79.

FOCAL TEXT

1 Corinthians 12:4–31a;
Ephesians 4:11–16;
1 Peter 4:10–11

BACKGROUND

Romans 12:1–8;
1 Corinthians 12;
Ephesians 4:1–16;
1 Peter 4:10–11

LESSON TWELVE

Be Generous with Your Gifts

MAIN IDEA

Christians are to use generously each gift God has given them, so as to provide for unity and effectiveness in the body of Christ and bring glory to God.

QUESTION TO EXPLORE

To what extent do you use generously the gifts God has given you?

STUDY AIM

To decide how I will use my gifts generously for the unity and effectiveness of the body of Christ and so bring glory to God

QUICK READ

The Spirit is the source of the variety of spiritual gifts. They are given to the Body of Christ for the purpose of service so as to glorify God.

Gus felt called to ministry at an early age and later was educated accordingly. After a hard divorce he decided to pursue business management. A lawsuit against his business landed him in prison. There he later drew close to the Lord. After prison Gus became a loyal husband, father, and church member. He was reluctant when asked to teach an adult Sunday School class. Fighting his past, he accepted, considering this a calling from the Lord. Surprisingly, the class grew as members sensed that his lessons and poignant questions were drawn from a deep well of wisdom.

If asked why success occurred, Gus pointed to the Lord, saying, "We must get self out of the way and let the Spirit work." We, like Gus, might think we have little to give, but the Lord remains faithful if we will join him in ministry.

1 CORINTHIANS 12:4–31A

4 Now there are varieties of gifts, but the same Spirit; 5 and there are varieties of services, but the same Lord; 6 and there are varieties of activities, but it is the same God who activates all of them in everyone. 7 To each is given the manifestation of the Spirit for the common good. 8 To one is given through the Spirit the utterance of wisdom, and to another the utterance of knowledge according to the same Spirit, 9 to another faith by the same Spirit, to

another gifts of healing by the one Spirit, [10] to another the working of miracles, to another prophecy, to another the discernment of spirits, to another various kinds of tongues, to another the interpretation of tongues. [11] All these are activated by one and the same Spirit, who allots to each one individually just as the Spirit chooses.

[12] For just as the body is one and has many members, and all the members of the body, though many, are one body, so it is with Christ. [13] For in the one Spirit we were all baptized into one body—Jews or Greeks, slaves or free—and we were all made to drink of one Spirit.

[14] Indeed, the body does not consist of one member but of many. [15] If the foot would say, "Because I am not a hand, I do not belong to the body," that would not make it any less a part of the body. [16] And if the ear would say, "Because I am not an eye, I do not belong to the body," that would not make it any less a part of the body. [17] If the whole body were an eye, where would the hearing be? If the whole body were hearing, where would the sense of smell be? [18] But as it is, God arranged the members in the body, each one of them, as he chose. [19] If all were a single member, where would the body be? [20] As it is, there are many members, yet one body. [21] The eye cannot say to the hand, "I have no need of you," nor again the head to the feet, "I have no need of you." [22] On the contrary, the members of the body that seem to be weaker are indispensable, [23] and those members of the body that we think less honorable we clothe with greater

honor, and our less respectable members are treated with greater respect; 24 whereas our more respectable members do not need this. But God has so arranged the body, giving the greater honor to the inferior member, 25 that there may be no dissension within the body, but the members may have the same care for one another. 26 If one member suffers, all suffer together with it; if one member is honored, all rejoice together with it.

27 Now you are the body of Christ and individually members of it. 28 And God has appointed in the church first apostles, second prophets, third teachers; then deeds of power, then gifts of healing, forms of assistance, forms of leadership, various kinds of tongues. 29 Are all apostles? Are all prophets? Are all teachers? Do all work miracles? 30 Do all possess gifts of healing? Do all speak in tongues? Do all interpret? 31 But strive for the greater gifts.

Ephesians 4:11–16

11 The gifts he gave were that some would be apostles, some prophets, some evangelists, some pastors and teachers, 12 to equip the saints for the work of ministry, for building up the body of Christ, 13 until all of us come to the unity of the faith and of the knowledge of the Son of God, to maturity, to the measure of the full stature of Christ. 14 We must no longer be children, tossed to

and fro and blown about by every wind of doctrine, by people's trickery, by their craftiness in deceitful scheming. [15] But speaking the truth in love, we must grow up in every way into him who is the head, into Christ, [16] from whom the whole body, joined and knit together by every ligament with which it is equipped, as each part is working properly, promotes the body's growth in building itself up in love.

1 PETER 4:10–11

[10] Like good stewards of the manifold grace of God, serve one another with whatever gift each of you has received. [11] Whoever speaks must do so as one speaking the very words of God; whoever serves must do so with the strength that God supplies, so that God may be glorified in all things through Jesus Christ. To him belong the glory and the power forever and ever. Amen.

The Source of the Gifts (1 Cor. 12:4–11)

Paul did not define spiritual gifts in 1 Corinthians 12:1–11 but rather provided correction for the church's infatuation with certain gifts. Apparently a large number of its members believed that certain gifts (speaking in tongues, prophecy, wisdom, and knowledge) were more important than others (1 Corinthians 13:1–2). They looked down on gifts deemed insignificant, such as loving service, which Paul mandated in 1 Corinthians 14:1.

In verses 4–6, Paul taught that different gifts exist. He contrasted the diversity of the gifts with the unity found in God. Three couplets mentioning "gifts," "services," and "activities" are examples of "manifestations of the Spirit" (1 Cor. 12:7).[1] These couplets show that God works in structured ways to build up his people for generous service. This theme of service resounds in Ephesians 4:11, where Paul described gifts enabling certain believers to take up servant leadership (apostles, prophets, evangelists, pastors, and teachers). With the phrase "various activities," Paul described God as the source of empowerment for believers (1 Cor. 12:6). In the original language, the word for "activities," *energematon*, means *resultant effects*, which reveals Paul's purpose, that God is even in control of the effects of gifts of service.

Verses 7–10 teach that the Corinthians must lay aside their belief in honor-based gifts. Such a view of gifts as bringing honor to the individual were a key element in Greco-Roman culture. Rather the Corinthians must submit to "the manifestation of the Spirit for the common good," that is, a blessing for all (1 Cor. 12:7).

The Spirit is the source of the four gifts in verses 8–9. The gifts do not come with detailed descriptions and thus caution is in order if seeking to define them.

Paul insisted that unity is possible because all believers are united in Christ (12:13). In 1 Corinthians 12 Paul sought to unify the church by providing insight into the variety of gifts available for ministry in the church. The gifts in 1 Corinthians 12:8–10 show this variety, especially when considering their uses in the lives of the apostles.

For example, in the Book of Acts, the Apostle Paul at times received wisdom directly from God through visions or direct communication (Acts 16:8–10; 23:11). At other times, Paul went to ask the other church leaders (Acts 15:2–4) or had personal wisdom about God's will (Acts 15:36–40).

Regarding the gift of healing, Peter on one hand healed people miraculously (Acts 3:6; 9:32–34, 40–41), but Paul on the other hand referred favorably to Luke, the beloved physician. Healing, therefore, can be miraculous or through other means. Thus, gifts appear manifold in expression, according to "the manifold grace of God" (1 Pet. 4:10).

Likewise, the gift of knowledge does not negate responsible studying and using the wonderful resources God has made available. Neither should believers avoid the guidance of those whom God has blessed with educated knowledge (Acts 8:28–35).

Other gifts, such as prophecy, are seen in the Old Testament and take on various forms. Prophecy is manifested in the Old Testament both as *forth-telling* and *foretelling*. *Forth-telling* is seen as proclaiming the message of God to people, "Hear the word of the Lord . . ." (Jeremiah 2:4). The message was for the current situation, not for the future. *Foretelling* means the heralding of a future event.

In light of the varied expressions of the gifts of wisdom, healing, knowledge, and prophecy, other gifts are likely to vary as well.

Verse 11 indicates that the same Spirit works in all believers and produces the desired abilities in every one of them. Jealousy on the one hand and pride on the other hand are contrary to the Spirit's intent for the gifts. Since the Spirit is the source for and authority of the gifts, believers must be content with their gifts and promote unity. These grace-motivated abilities are a means to bless the whole church. This intent, however, does not exclude personal responsibility, study, or practice.

The Focus of the Gifts
(1 Cor. 12:12–31a; Eph. 4:11–16)

In 1 Corinthians 12:12–31, Paul used a powerful analogy to emphasize that members must promote unity rather than focus on personal benefit and divide the church. He portrayed the church as a human body, the Body of Christ. Regardless of their background (1 Cor. 12:13), all believers are brought together in Christ by God's Spirit. They are connected in Christ, as the parts of a body are all connected to the body (12:14). Christians function like members of the human body, working together to fulfill the will of Christ (12:15–21).

Paul further used his analogy of the body to show that all gifts are needed in the church. Much as each member of the human body is needed for proper functioning, so each believer is needed for the church to fulfill its intended purpose (12:14–26). Only when believers work together in perfect synergy does the church experience unity and are gifts used for their intended purpose.

Paul's humor in verses 15–21 is corrective. Immaturity in the Corinthian church was exposed through the personification of body parts. Body parts revolt and say they have no use for other body parts. How will the feet, the ears, or the eyes function by themselves? The absurdity is the point. Church members are weak without all members working together. Greater honor to parts seemingly weaker or less honorable is most appropriate (12:23–24). This recognition of the lowly is reminiscent of Jesus' description of the kingdom (Matt. 23:11–12). God has given greater honor to those appearing insignificant. God through Christ uses every gift for the total health of the body and the working of his will.

God has appointed church leaders as well (1 Cor. 12:28). Apostles are listed as appointed first, prophets second, teachers third, followed by gifts of power, healing, assistance (service), forms of leadership, and tongues (12:28). Paul next rhetorically asked whether all are apostles, prophets, or teachers, and whether all work miracles, have gifts of healing, speak in tongues, or interpret (12:29–30). In the original language, the reply to the question was part of the question—a negative answer was expected. The expected answer was, *No, they are not all apostles, prophets, or teachers, and they do not all have these gifts.*

In the Letter to the Ephesians, Paul likewise described healthy functioning of the church by using the metaphor of the body. In the list of gifts mentioned in Ephesians, apostles and prophets are listed in a similar order as they were presented in 1 Corinthians 12 (Eph. 4:11). Certain other gifts are mentioned in Ephesians that do not occur in 1 Corinthians 12. In Ephesians 4:11, following prophets, Paul included evangelists, pastors, and teachers.

What is essential to observe is the focus of the gifts. The leadership-oriented gifts listed in Ephesians and their counterparts in the church in Corinth specifically are intended to build up of the Body of Christ (Eph. 4:12–16). Likewise other gifts are for the mutual good of believers and are thus for the entire church (1 Cor. 12: 25–26).

The Purpose of the Gifts (1 Pet. 4:10–11)

In 1 Peter 4 believers are exhorted not to live like people in the world (1 Peter 4:1–3). Those in the world who live a lifestyle of sin will ultimately give an account before the heavenly judge (1 Pet. 4:5).

Starting with verse 7, the focus is futuristic. "The end of all things is near" (4:7). Using this perspective as a motivator, believers were exhorted to live a disciplined life. This lifestyle requires constant love among believers, for such love covers any sins committed that might have disturbed the fellowship (4:8). Hesitation to offer hospitality to other Christians (in this case likely traveling preachers) might have led to broken relationships. Verse 9 calls for hospitality.

The believers were reminded to serve by using the gifts each had received (4:10). The use of these gifts for service is an outflow of the stewardship of God's "manifold grace" (4:10), referring to the grace of the God who works in unity and creates great diversity. Verse 10 infers that each member's gift is a result of grace and hence God's generosity.

Whoever speaks must recognize the source of the words—God. This speaking likely refers to preaching the word of God. The intent of the text is sober teaching, teaching that avoids opinions and speculation. Believers are instructed to remember "the words of God" rather than to wander into unfounded opinions. Rather, God's words were to be studied and then applied (4:11). Likewise, those who serve must do so in God's strength (4:11). By using God's strength, God is glorified. Thus, by using the spiritual gifts for service, God is glorified in Christ (4:11).

Implications and Actions

Christians are called to use their God-given gifts with great care. The church is effective as the Body of Christ in the world only when maintaining unity and encouraging generosity in the use of gifts. God has given gifts that, although great in variety, derive all from the same Spirit. Too, believers must remember that gifts are not intended to bless one but to bless all.

Contentment with the Spirit's giving of gifts is the only reasonable response of all believers. These grace-filled gifts never should incite pride but edification. In the exercise of gifts, believers should seek to use their gifts for the building up of the whole church. Furthermore, all the gifts are valuable and, if used responsibly and generously, produce God's intended effects in the church for God's glory.

THE BODY

Paul referred to the Corinthian church with metaphors that were familiar concepts in the culture—a field (1 Cor. 3:5–9), a building (3:9–15), and a human body (12:12–31). The body metaphor was used widely in political speeches of the time.[2] The Roman senate, for example, was compared to a head, while the people were compared to a body.

Additionally, as the Romans later carried out building programs throughout their empire, this Greek influence still was visible in their art. For example, archaeological finds at Ephesus (in modern Turkey) and at Caesarea Maritima (at the coast of Israel) include large sculptures of feet, ears, eyes, and other body parts and organs. Paul used body and body parts imagery in his explanation of the functioning of the church. With Corinth located in Greece in the Roman Empire, the metaphor spoke loudly and clearly to the believers' imagination and hearts.

QUESTIONS

1. Read Romans 12:5. What does it mean practically to be "individually . . . members one of another"?

2. Why would the more service-oriented gifts not have
   been viewed as most desired among the Corinthian
   believers? Is this trend still observed today in the
   churches? Why? Why not?

3. What are forms of forth-telling today?

4. In what sense does love cover sin? Can you share a personal experience that exemplifies this truth?

NOTES

1. Gordon D. Fee, *The New International Commentary on the New Testament: The First Epistle to the Corinthians* (Grand Rapids, MI: William B. Eerdmans, 1987), 589.

2. David E. Garland, *Baker Exegetical Commentary on the New Testament: 1 Corinthians* (Grand Rapids, MI: Baker Academics, 2003), 588–589.

FOCAL TEXT

Luke 21:1–4;
1 Timothy 6:6–10, 17–19

BACKGROUND

Luke 21:1–4; 1 Timothy 6

LESSON THIRTEEN

Be Generous with Your Money

MAIN IDEA

Since God richly provides for us, Christians are to be generous with their money and ready to share it, rather than loving it, hoarding it for themselves, and trusting in it.

QUESTION TO EXPLORE

How can we determine when we value money and material possessions too much?

STUDY AIM

To decide to give of my material resources more generously

QUICK READ

Generous people give themselves. Too, they do not give from their overflow but from their subsistence. They are content, have proper priorities, and joyfully give of their material resources.

In February of 1812, two ships departed from Philadelphia carrying newly commissioned Congregationalist missionaries Adoniram Judson and Luther Rice to India. As they sailed, neither man knew that both of them were studying the Greek New Testament and simultaneously were becoming Baptist in beliefs. After arriving in Asia, Rice was chosen to return to New York in order to break ties with the Congregationalists and establish a relationship with the Baptists.

Rice could never have imagined that he would not marry the woman he loved and that he would give the remaining twenty-four years of his life to raising funds for international missions. Owning only his clothing and horse, Columbus, he traveled "from Maine to Georgia and even across the Appalachians," dealing with heat and cold, through mountains, ice cold rivers, and hostile lands. His only goal was to preach the gospel and to provide support to missionaries to reach the lost in foreign lands. At the time of his death in 1846, his vision for missions had succeeded. God had moved Baptists to support generously numerous missions, missionaries, and schools of higher education.[1]

This lesson's passages discuss true generosity. From the life and ministry of Christ, we will first study that true generosity gives of self. Then we will learn from 1 Timothy 6 that such generosity displays contentment and proper priorities.

LUKE 21:1–4

[1] He looked up and saw rich people putting their gifts into the treasury; [2] he also saw a poor widow put in two small copper coins. [3] He said, "Truly I tell you, this poor widow has put in more than all of them; [4] for all of them have contributed out of their abundance, but she out of her poverty has put in all she had to live on."

1 TIMOTHY 6:6–10, 17–19

[6] Of course, there is great gain in godliness combined with contentment; [7] for we brought nothing into the world, so that we can take nothing out of it; [8] but If we have food and clothing, we will be content with these. [9] But those who want to be rich fall into temptation and are trapped by many senseless and harmful desires that plunge people into ruin and destruction. [10] For the love of money is a root of all kinds of evil, and in their eagerness to be rich some have wandered away from the faith and pierced themselves with many pains.

• •

[17] As for those who in the present age are rich, command them not to be haughty, or to set their hopes on the uncertainty of riches, but rather on God who richly provides us with everything for our enjoyment. [18] They

are to do good, to be rich in good works, generous, and ready to share, [19] thus storing up for themselves the treasure of a good foundation for the future, so that they may take hold of the life that really is life.

True Generosity Gives of Self (Luke 21:1–4)

The best understanding of Luke's account of Jesus and the widow's temple gift starts by considering the events leading up to that passage. In Luke 19, Jesus entered Jerusalem while the multitudes proclaimed, "Blessed is the king who comes in the name of the Lord! Peace in heaven, and glory in the highest heaven" (Luke 19:38). Luke describes the angry reaction of the Pharisees and their resulting command to Jesus to stop the crowd's praise (19:39). Next, Jesus entered the Jerusalem temple. There Jesus drove out the sellers and declared the temple a den of robbers (19:45).

Luke 20 narrates Jesus' teachings in the temple. The chapter tells of Jesus' confrontations with the temple's religious leaders. The scribes and the chief priests attempted to ambush Jesus by asking him a question regarding the necessity of paying taxes to Caesar (20:19–26). At that moment, these leaders cared little about tax matters but only about trying to discredit Jesus. Next, the Sadducees equally tried to set up Jesus by presenting him with a predicament about the resurrection (20:27–40). Jesus perceived their intent and shamed them before the crowds.

He then posed a question to the religious leaders that evidenced his identity as the Messiah (20:41–44). Next, Jesus warned the people about the scribes (20:45–47). He described them as people in lavish clothing who adored praise, and he exposed their practice of taking "widow's houses." The scribes had created a loophole in the Hebrew law. That is, upon the death of her husband a widow did not have rights to the inheritance. Widows had little means of support and were incredibly vulnerable.[2] Jesus charged that the leaders' encouragement of exploitation (see also Matthew 15:5) caused shameful oppression in society.[3]

Jesus' warning against the scribes' terrible treatment of widows forms the backdrop to the next episode in Luke's account. Luke ensures that the reader stores in mind Jesus' denunciation of the leaders who devoured widows' houses. In the very next incident, a poor widow appeared on the scene. By stating in Luke 21:1, "He [Jesus] looked up and . . . ," Luke joins the coming episode with the plight of Israel's widows (Luke 20:45–47).

In Luke 21:1–4, Jesus was observing people bringing gifts to the temple treasury. Rich people brought notable gifts, but Luke describes the poor widow's tiny gift in detail. She brought two small copper coins (21:2), *lepta*, the smallest coins in circulation.[4] Jesus pointed out the contrast in giving. The gifts of the rich were substantial, and the gift of the poor widow was comparatively insignificant in monetary amount (21:4). The widow's gift, though, was great because she gave out of all that she had (21:4). In the original language, the word *bios* is used, which is best translated as *life*. Thus, she gave of her very *life* or sustenance!

Two aspects of generosity can be derived from this passage in Luke. First of all, our generosity should never come at another person's expense and especially not at the expense of those who need our care. The temple leaders exploited the widows in society, the very people their administration should have been protecting. They greedily took the widows' only property and sacrificial gifts. The amount they extracted was only a fraction of their own great wealth. Jesus reprimanded them with harsh words, words we must heed today.

We ought never to squeeze every drop out of the vulnerable in the gimmicks that build only earthly kingdoms and comforts. Rather, we must care for the vulnerable ones, making sure they thrive. Secondly, we ought to understand God's kingdom values as symbolized by the poor widow. She gave of her *life*, a generosity that reveals love toward others and not simply attention to customs. She shared her meager sustenance with others.[5] As participants in God's kingdom, we are to share of ourselves and our very sustenance with heartfelt generosity.

True Generosity Knows Contentment (1 Tim. 6:6–10)

Chapter 6 in 1 Timothy begins with a warning against false teachers. They believed that godly living was a way to get rich (1 Tim. 6:5). Verse 6 corrects these errors. "Godliness" is "gain," but not in a monetary sense. It is "gain" only if combined with "contentment" (6:6). In verse 6, the term "gain" is used in a metaphorical sense and is contrasted with the preceding verse. The Greek word translated "contentment," *autarkia,* was used by Greek philosophers and expressed the idea of self-sufficiency. However, Paul here envisioned *Christ-sufficiency.*[6]

Verse 7 reminds us, "we brought nothing into the world, so that we can take nothing out of it." Thus we should be grateful for and content with the basic necessities of life, such as food and clothing (6:8). This gratefulness, or contentment, is contrasted in verse 8 with greed in verse 9. Those who want riches rather than contentment give in to temptations and end up in ruin and destruction.

Paul described a slippery slope of greed. First, greedy people (those who want to get rich) fall into temptation, which leads to entrapment by many senseless and harmless desires. Finally, these desires plunge the greedy "into ruin and destruction" (6:9).

In verse 10, Paul continued to explain what happens when contentment gives way to greed. Referring in verse 9 to the slippery slope—or the downward spiral—of "evil," Paul pointed out that "the love of money is a root of all kinds of evil" (6:10). The word "root" does not have an article in the original language and thus is to be understood as *one of the roots* of all evil. Nevertheless, this root, the love of money, is powerful. The pursuit of riches can lead to temptation. In the Old Testament, the very possession of wealth led to temptation (see Proverbs 11:4, 16, 28; 23:4–5; Ecclesiastes 5:12–13).[7] In the end, materialism can lead believers away from their faith, whereas contentment with the things provided by God leads to a deeper faith experience.

True Generosity Knows Right Priorities (1 Tim. 6:17–19)

In 1 Timothy 6:17, Paul stated as a command that the rich were not to be haughty, adding that command to the call for contentment given in verse 6. Some people not only were discontent or greedy, but they also actually deemed themselves better than others because of their riches. Paul told Timothy to command them to stop doing that (1 Tim. 6:17).

Paul described the rich people who had this pride problem connected to their money as those who are rich "in the present age" (6:17). Thus, Paul clearly demarcated present life (life on earth) from the life to come (heavenly life). The rich believers had set their hope on "the uncertainty of riches," a future-oriented hope focused on the wrong object (6:17). They needed to set their hope on God and not on riches (6:17). God provides believers with security, not the riches of this world (6:17).

"The present age" refers to life lived in a society not always accommodating to the values of God's kingdom. In Ephesians 1:21 Paul wrote of "this age but also . . . the one to come." The one to come is the age of the full reign of God in Christ (Revelation 11:15). The believers were to set their hope in this present age on the same values as in the world to come, which is the rule and reign of Christ.

The virtues in verse 18 are presented as alternative actions to placing trust in riches. Rather than looking down on those who do not have similar financial means, those who are rich in this world are to do good, find their riches in doing good works, and have a generous heart that is willing to share. Believers who focus on the features described in verse 18 invest in the future (6:19). They have their priorities in order. Riches are invested in a foundation for the future, the things of God, rather than in earthly enjoyment. Those who store up the treasure of a good foundation "may take hold of the life that really is" (6:19). The life "that really is" can be experienced in this earthly life when our focus is on God.

Implications and Actions

The Lord looks at the heart when people give. Because the Lord views the heart, he knows when people are suffering financial abuse or financial need. Consequently, Christians are responsible to address abuse and to generously meet needs. Christ's sacrifice on the cross reveals the depths to which we should be willing to go in our giving and serving. Greed has no part in the Christian's life.

Generous believers should realize that giving is more than a custom. Giving is a loving response to the love of our Lord. We must be wise in finances so we can be generous in the church and provide for the needy. Christ's suffering should eradicate greed from our hearts and prompt generosity in all areas of life. Financial responsibility and faithful giving should be evident in our daily lives. Generous people are content, have proper priorities, and joyfully give of their material resources.

LIMITED GOOD, SHARING, AND WEALTH

Economics in the Bible world varied greatly from concepts about finances in today's Western society. People in Bible times viewed the goods of life as limited in supply, as expressed in this statement: *There is only a limited amount of this where this came from.* This is called *limited good.* If someone gained goods, it was at the presumed expense of others.[8] In the West, the perception of goods is: *There is always more where this came from.*

To the ancients everything existed within a closed system. The peasants lived in a system of heavy taxation by the wealthy elite, who controlled the resources and power in society. Limited supplies were divided among the people in the villages and communities who shared their goods.[9] Holding back from such supplies by storing up goods for private use or storing treasures in the ground depleted the perceived limited amount of goods—agricultural products and money.

Followers of Jesus shared everything and provided for the needy (Acts 2:44–45). During Jesus' ministry, followers provided for the proclamation of God's kingdom (Luke 8:1–3). At times, churches failed to do so, and even Paul went hungry (Philippians 4:12, 15). Christians, however, are to share generously and joyfully.

TREASURES

In New Testament times, people typically stored their riches in the ground. If a soldier left for war, he would hide his treasure in the field. However, at times he would not return from war. Since no one else knew the location of the treasure, it would remain hidden in the field until someone might find it by accident. Those who wanted to use their means for immediate use, such as buying land, would dig up their own treasure to use for that purpose.

QUESTIONS

1. Have you ever witnessed a real-life equivalent to the story of the widow and her gift? How did that make you feel? Did it change you? If so, how? If not, why not?

2. In what ways can the church help the needy within it?

3. In what ways did Jesus exemplify godliness combined with contentment?

4. What are some practical examples of what godliness combined with contentment looks like in the life of a believer?

5. Would you say that the vast majority of American Christians fit the description "rich in this present world" compared to the rest of the people of the world? How then should this translate into generosity in American churches? Does it? Why or why not?

6. When does one cross the line between being responsible with money and placing one's security and hope in one's financial means?

7. Can one ever be too generous? Why? Why not?

NOTES

1. http://www.beesondivinity.com/howoldarethebaptists. Accessed 1/12/12.

2. Craig Keener, *The IVP Bible Background Commentary: New Testament* (Downers Grove, IL: InterVarsity Press, 1993), 238, 246.

3. Bruce J. Malina and Richard L. Rohrbaugh, *Social-Science Commentary on the Synoptic Gospels*, 2nd edition (Minneapolis, MN: Fortress Press, 2003), 423.

4. Luke Timothy Johnson, *Sacra Pagina: Luke*, vol. 3 (Collegeville, MN: The Liturgical Press, 1991), 316.

5. Johnson, 319.

6. Gordon D. Fee, *New International Biblical Commentary: 1 and 2 Timothy, Titus*, vol. 13 (Peabody, MA: Hendrickson Publishers,1988), 143.

7. William D. Mounce, *Word Biblical Commentary: Pastoral Epistles*, vol. 46 (Nashville, TN: Thomas Nelson Publishers, 2000), 346.

8. K.C. Hanson and Douglas E. Oakman, *Palestine in the Time of Jesus: Social Structures and Social Conflicts*, 2nd edition (Minneapolis, MN: Fortress Press, 2008), 103.

9. John J. Pilch and Bruce J. Malina, eds., *Handbook of Biblical Social Values* (Peabody, MA: Hendrickson Publishers, Inc., 1998), 123.

Our Next New Study
(Available for use beginning September 2012)

THE BOOK OF ACTS:
Time to Act on Acts 1:8

Additional Future Adult Study

The Gospel of Mark: People   For use beginning
Responding to Jesus   December 2012

How to Order More Bible Study Materials

It's easy! Just fill in the following information. For additional Bible study materials available both in print and online, see www.baptistwaypress.org, or get a complete order form of available print materials—including Spanish materials—by calling 1-866-249-1799 or e-mailing baptistway@texasbaptists.org.

Title of item	Price	Quantity	Cost
This Issue:			
Living Generously for Jesus' Sake—Study Guide (BWP001137)	$3.95	_____	_____
Living Generously for Jesus' Sake—Large Print Study Guide (BWP001138)	$4.25	_____	_____
Living Generously for Jesus' Sake—Teaching Guide (BWP001139)	$4.95	_____	_____
Additional Issues Available:			
Growing Together in Christ—Study Guide (BWP001036)	$3.25	_____	_____
Growing Together in Christ—Teaching Guide (BWP001038)	$3.75	_____	_____
Living Faith in Daily Life—Study Guide (BWP001095)	$3.55	_____	_____
Living Faith in Daily Life—Large Print Study Guide (BWP001096)	$3.95	_____	_____
Living Faith in Daily Life—Teaching Guide (BWP001097)	$4.25	_____	_____
Participating in God's Mission—Study Guide (BWP001077)	$3.55	_____	_____
Participating in God's Mission—Large Print Study Guide (BWP001078)	$3.95	_____	_____
Participating in God's Mission—Teaching Guide (BWP001079)	$3.55	_____	_____
Profiles in Character—Study Guide (BWP001112)	$3.55	_____	_____
Profiles in Character—Large Print Study Guide (BWP001113)	$4.25	_____	_____
Profiles in Character—Teaching Guide (BWP001114)	$4.95	_____	_____
Genesis: People Relating to God—Study Guide (BWP001088)	$2.35	_____	_____
Genesis: People Relating to God—Large Print Study Guide (BWP001089)	$2.75	_____	_____
Genesis: People Relating to God—Teaching Guide (BWP001090)	$2.95	_____	_____
Genesis 12—50: Family Matters—Study Guide (BWP000034)	$1.95	_____	_____
Genesis 12—50: Family Matters—Teaching Guide (BWP000035)	$2.45	_____	_____
Leviticus, Numbers, Deuteronomy—Study Guide (BWP000053)	$2.35	_____	_____
Leviticus, Numbers, Deuteronomy—Large Print Study Guide (BWP000052)	$2.35	_____	_____
Leviticus, Numbers, Deuteronomy—Teaching Guide (BWP000054)	$2.95	_____	_____
1 and 2 Samuel—Study Guide (BWP000002)	$2.35	_____	_____
1 and 2 Samuel—Large Print Study Guide (BWP000001)	$2.35	_____	_____
1 and 2 Samuel—Teaching Guide (BWP000003)	$2.95	_____	_____
1 and 2 Kings: Leaders and Followers—Study Guide (BWP001025)	$2.95	_____	_____
1 and 2 Kings: Leaders and Followers Large Print Study Guide (BWP001026)	$3.15	_____	_____
1 and 2 Kings: Leaders and Followers Teaching Guide (BWP001027)	$3.45	_____	_____
Ezra, Haggai, Zechariah, Nehemiah, Malachi—Study Guide (BWP001071)	$3.25	_____	_____
Ezra, Haggai, Zechariah, Nehemiah, Malachi—Large Print Study Guide (BWP001072)	$3.55	_____	_____
Ezra, Haggai, Zechariah, Nehemiah, Malachi—Teaching Guide (BWP001073)	$3.75	_____	_____
Job, Ecclesiastes, Habakkuk, Lamentations—Study Guide (BWP001016)	$2.75	_____	_____
Job, Ecclesiastes, Habakkuk, Lamentations—Large Print Study Guide (BWP001017)	$2.85	_____	_____
Job, Ecclesiastes, Habakkuk, Lamentations—Teaching Guide (BWP001018)	$3.25	_____	_____
Psalms and Proverbs—Study Guide (BWP001000)	$2.75	_____	_____
Psalms and Proverbs—Teaching Guide (BWP001002)	$3.25	_____	_____
Amos, Hosea, Isaiah, Micah: Calling for Justice, Mercy, and Faithfulness—Study Guide (BWP001132)	$3.95	_____	_____
Amos, Hosea, Isaiah, Micah: Calling for Justice, Mercy, and Faithfulness—Large Print Study Guide (BWP001133)	$4.25	_____	_____
Amos, Hosea, Isaiah, Micah: Calling for Justice, Mercy, and Faithfulness—Teaching Guide (BWP001134)	$4.95	_____	_____
The Gospel of Matthew: A Primer for Discipleship—Study Guide (BWP001127)	$3.95	_____	_____
The Gospel of Matthew: A Primer for Discipleship—Large Print Study Guide (BWP001128)	$4.25	_____	_____
The Gospel of Matthew: A Primer for Discipleship—Teaching Guide (BWP001129)	$4.95	_____	_____
Matthew: Hope in the Resurrected Christ—Study Guide (BWP001066)	$3.25	_____	_____
Matthew: Hope in the Resurrected Christ—Large Print Study Guide (BWP001067)	$3.55	_____	_____
Matthew: Hope in the Resurrected Christ—Teaching Guide (BWP001068)	$3.75	_____	_____
Mark: Jesus' Works and Words—Study Guide (BWP001022)	$2.95	_____	_____
Mark: Jesus' Works and Words—Large Print Study Guide (BWP001023)	$3.15	_____	_____
Mark:Jesus' Works and Words—Teaching Guide (BWP001024)	$3.45	_____	_____
Jesus in the Gospel of Mark—Study Guide (BWP000066)	$1.95	_____	_____
Jesus in the Gospel of Mark—Teaching Guide (BWP000067)	$2.45	_____	_____
Luke: Journeying to the Cross—Study Guide (BWP000057)	$2.35	_____	_____
Luke: Journeying to the Cross—Large Print Study Guide (BWP000056)	$2.35	_____	_____
Luke: Journeying to the Cross—Teaching Guide (BWP000058)	$2.95	_____	_____
The Gospel of John: Light Overcoming Darkness, Part One—Study Guide (BWP001104)	$3.55	_____	_____
The Gospel of John: Light Overcoming Darkness, Part One—Large Print Study Guide (BWP001105)	$3.95	_____	_____
The Gospel of John: Light Overcoming Darkness, Part One—Teaching Guide (BWP001106)	$4.50	_____	_____
The Gospel of John: Light Overcoming Darkness, Part Two—Study Guide (BWP001109)	$3.55	_____	_____
The Gospel of John: Light Overcoming Darkness, Part Two—Large Print Study Guide (BWP001110)	$3.95	_____	_____
The Gospel of John: Light Overcoming Darkness, Part Two—Teaching Guide (BWP001111)	$4.50	_____	_____
The Gospel of John: The Word Became Flesh—Study Guide (BWP001008)	$2.75	_____	_____
The Gospel of John: The Word Became Flesh—Large Print Study Guide (BWP001009)	$2.85	_____	_____
The Gospel of John: The Word Became Flesh—Teaching Guide (BWP001010)	$3.25	_____	_____

Acts: Toward Being a Missional Church—Study Guide (BWP001013) $2.75 _____ _____
Acts: Toward Being a Missional Church—Large Print Study Guide (BWP001014) $2.85 _____ _____
Acts: Toward Being a Missional Church—Teaching Guide (BWP001015) $3.25 _____ _____
Romans: What God Is Up To—Study Guide (BWP001019) $2.95 _____ _____
Romans: What God Is Up To—Large Print Study Guide (BWP001020) $3.15 _____ _____
Romans: What God Is Up To—Teaching Guide (BWP001021) $3.45 _____ _____
The Corinthian Letters—Study Guide (BWP001121) $3.55 _____ _____
The Corinthian Letters—Large Print Study Guide (BWP001122) $4.25 _____ _____
The Corinthian Letters—Teaching Guide (BWP001123) $4.95 _____ _____
Galatians and 1&2 Thessalonians—Study Guide (BWP001080) $3.55 _____ _____
Galatians and 1&2 Thessalonians—Large Print Study Guide (BWP001081) $3.95 _____ _____
Galatians and 1&2 Thessalonians—Teaching Guide (BWP001082) $3.95 _____ _____
1, 2 Timothy, Titus, Philemon—Study Guide (BWP000092) $2.75 _____ _____
1, 2 Timothy, Titus, Philemon—Teaching Guide (BWP000093) $3.25 _____ _____
Letters of James and John—Study Guide (BWP001101) $3.55 _____ _____
Letters of James and John—Large Print Study Guide (BWP001102) $3.95 _____ _____
Letters of James and John—Teaching Guide (BWP001103) $4.25 _____ _____

Coming for use beginning September 2012

The Book of Acts: Time to Act on Acts 1:8—Study Guide (BWP001142) $3.95 _____ _____
The Book of Acts: Time to Act on Acts 1:8—Large Print Study Guide (BWP001143) $4.25 _____ _____
The Book of Acts: Time to Act on Acts 1:8—Teaching Guide (BWP001144) $4.95 _____ _____

Standard (UPS/Mail) Shipping Charges*			
Order Value	Shipping charge**	Order Value	Shipping charge**
$.01—$9.99	$6.50	$160.00—$199.99	$24.00
$10.00—$19.99	$8.50	$200.00—$249.99	$28.00
$20.00—$39.99	$9.50	$250.00—$299.99	$30.00
$40.00—$59.99	$10.50	$300.00—$349.99	$34.00
$60.00—$79.99	$11.50	$350.00—$399.99	$42.00
$80.00—$99.99	$12.50	$400.00—$499.99	$50.00
$100.00—$129.99	$15.00	$500.00—$599.99	$60.00
$130.00—$159.99	$20.00	$600.00—$799.99	$72.00**

Cost of items (Order value) _____

Shipping charges (see chart*) _____

TOTAL _____

*Plus, applicable taxes for individuals and other taxable entities (not churches) within Texas will be added. Please call 1-866-249-1799 if the exact amount is needed prior to ordering.

**For order values $800.00 and above, please call 1-866-249-1799 or check www.baptistwaypress.org

Please allow three weeks for standard delivery. For express shipping service: Call 1-866-249-1799 for information on additional charges.

YOUR NAME _____

PHONE _____

YOUR CHURCH _____

DATE ORDERED _____

SHIPPING ADDRESS _____

CITY _____

STATE _____ ZIP CODE _____

E-MAIL _____

MAIL this form with your check for the total amount to
BAPTISTWAY PRESS, Baptist General Convention of Texas,
333 North Washington, Dallas, TX 75246-1798
(Make checks to "Baptist Executive Board.")

OR, **FAX** your order anytime to: 214-828-5376, and we will bill you.

OR, **CALL** your order toll-free: 1-866-249-1799
(M-Fri 8:30 a.m.-5:00 p.m. central time), and we will bill you.

OR, **E-MAIL** your order to our internet e-mail address:
baptistway@texasbaptists.org, and we will bill you.

OR, **ORDER ONLINE** at www.baptistwaypress.org.

We look forward to receiving your order! Thank you!